THE
CENTURION

THE CENTURION

and other religious plays

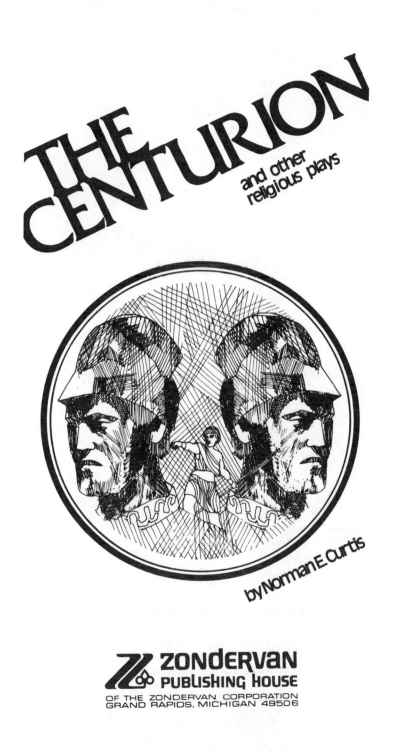

by Norman E. Curtis

Z ZONDERVAN PUBLISHING HOUSE

OF THE ZONDERVAN CORPORATION
GRAND RAPIDS, MICHIGAN 49506

Contents

THE CENTURION

THE CENTURION

Characters

Narrator
Flavius— the Centurion
Caesar — Emperor of Rome
Pilate — Procurator of Judea
Innkeeper — elderly owner of inn in Bethlehem
Julian — innkeeper's son (about forty)
Tobias — aged shepherd
Herod — King of Galilee
John the Baptist
Nicodemus — Jewish leader
Mary — mother of Jesus
Mary Magdalene
Mary Cleophas
John — the disciple
Caiaphas — a high priest
Barabbas — prisoner released in place of Jesus
Longinus — a Roman soldier
Two guards
Women — 1, 2, 3, 4, 5
Men — 1, 2, 3, 4
Priests — 1, 2
Roman soldiers — four or six
Crowd — men and women
Voices — Jesus and two thieves

Time

Day of Christ's crucifixion, with flashbacks to other times

Place

Golgotha, with flashbacks to other settings

This drama may be performed with or without scenery, costumes, and lights, depending upon the physical facilities available or the artistic desires of the director.

7

Naturally costumes, scenery, and lighting add much to any production, but at times striking effects and excellent results are to be derived from a presentation which utilizes the pantomime, speech, and pacing of a well-directed and talented cast, using a bare stage and limited lighting. This drama is designed to be adapted to any form of presentation without weakening the message it offers.

The director may use a single-level stage divided into three areas of action, or, if facilities warrant, three levels of action as shown in Fig. 1. Spotlighted each area of action so that each area can be illuminated separately from the others will cause the action not only to move smoothly, but will also give the illusion of separate scenes. Even on a single-level stage separate lighting of the three areas of action can contribute greatly to establishing the effect of scene shifting.

Whichever presentation is used, the director should adapt to the physical plant available and to the quality of the cast to present the drama to advantage. Putting most of the effort into the pantomime and speaking of lines, it will prove a most worthwhile project for any group.

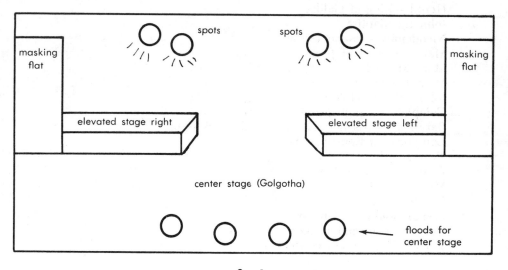

fig. 1

Suggestions and Preparations

Study Fig. 1. The lighting, as shown, should be capable of illuminating only the immediate area. In this way, a sense of scene change will be effected.

The center acting area is always the summit of Golgotha, while the two elevated areas depict the many scenes as they occur in the drama apart from the crucifixion. When lighting is used, it should be coor-

8

dinated so that as one scene fades, the next scene comes up, with the actors in position and acting. Flavius is always in the dark when addressing the other scenes, and the actors in those scenes always speak directly to him, even though he may not be seen distinctly. Flavius always faces the scene to which he is speaking.

The three crosses are directly above the audience. They are not visible to anyone, but the illusion that they are there is created as everyone in the Golgotha scene looks up at them, imagining they actually see them. It is best to select a specific spot for everyone to look at when referring to them. Flavius must be especially aware of where he looks, as he is in constant "contact" with the center cross. The crowd at the Golgotha scene is at all times aware of the crosses.

It would be effective to have a constant, low hum of crowd sounds whenever the Golgotha scene is lighted. This only falls silent at particular times in the scenes when silence is indicated. This will necessitate a low, almost deliberate "conversation" between those who are not engaged in actual dialogue at the moment, but it must come from them naturally, as if discussing the crosses. In it are mingled glances and occasional gestures toward the crosses.

However, "conversation" and gestures must not interfere with or detract from the dialogue that is carrying the story line. When the action shifts to the other two areas, the people in the center scene must be motionless and silent until the action shifts back to them.

All entrances must be made with careful attention to dramatic intent to avoid the appearance of merely getting into position to deliver lines. In the event that the drama is presented without special lighting or divided stage, it is best for the entire cast to arrange themselves in an orderly position upstage and step forward into the scenes as they appear.

One person could play several parts — all that is needed is to interpret each character with an identifying pantomine or speech pattern. An imaginative director is able to create many personalities with a few performers if great care is given to these matters.

Finally, it is always best to have all dialogue memorized, but THE CENTURION can be effectively presented as a reading. Care must be given to the manner in which each line is read, however, to create the illusion of scenes and characters.

Note 1: To make the production attractive and effective, the masking flats may be constructed to appear as huge boulders and the elevated stages as flat promontories atop Golgotha. Added interest may be included by varying the colors and intensities of the lighting of these secondary levels. If at all possible, the entire scene can be made to have unlimited depth by the addition of a blue cyclorama, referred to in theater parlance as a "Sky-Cyc."

The stage blocking should be set so that no one participating in the Golgotha scene is ever allowed to be in an upright position before either of the elevated stages when a scene is being enacted thereon. This will eliminate confusion on the part of the viewers as to the separation of scenes.

Note 2: If the Centurion's voice needs to be augmented when his back is to the audience, one microphone suspended upstage and well above him will suffice. It is best to choose a Centurion whose voice needs no amplification, even when his back is to the audience, rather than to be faced with the necessity of having twentieth century equipment hanging in a first century setting. However, whatever is necessary to bring intelligible and effective dialogue to your audience should be your primary concern.

NARR: The time is shortly past noon on a day nearly 2,000 years ago. The place is a rocky hill, just outside the walls of Jerusalem, which is called Golgotha or "The Place of the Skull." At the summit of this craggy promontory, overlooking the city, three crosses stand silhouetted against a sun-drenched sky. Upon each cross is nailed a human form.

The center figure is quiet; there is little movement. The two on either side writhe in agony. On the ground below a crowd has gathered made up of people usually found at such occasions: the jeering, faceless majority; the sadist who revels in inhuman cruelty; the curious who either stand and gape or leave quickly, their faces mirroring the horror they have witnessed; those who have come to see "justice" done; the few who taunt the helpless victims and torment them with stones; and the passer-by who goes out of his way to catch a glimpse of the macabre.

At such a spectacle there are usually sympathizers and sorrowing relatives, and this is no exception, for there are many such gathered at the foot of the center cross. In this instance they are mostly women, with only two or three men in evidence.

The Roman soldiers have just finished their task and are at the moment dividing the garments of the crucified among themselves. To one side, strangely present at such a scene, stand a number of priests from the temple.

Directly beneath the center cross, looking up at the suffering form hanging there, stands a Roman officer, a Centurion. Apparently he is in charge, but at the moment he is studying the face of the central figure.

(*As Narrator speaks the closing lines, a dim spot comes up on the Centurion's face. The crowd noise begins. The spot remains dim for a few moments and then slowly the lights come up to full on the center area of the stage.*

To the left of the Centurion are a number of soldiers dividing the garments. Behind them is a group of men and women who are taunting the victims. Center stage, behind the Centurion, are the priests. To the right of them are a number of curiosity seekers. Directly to the right of the Centurion are the three Marys, John, and a number of men and women who are comforting Mary, the mother of Jesus, and other sorrowing friends. The Centurion is silent for a few moments; then he looks at the jeering crowd that is edging to the front. He speaks to Longinus, one of the soldiers, who snaps to attention.)

CENT: Longinus, I want you to keep this crowd back. As soon as you have divided those garments, see to it that no one goes beyond that line!

LONG: *(Saluting with clenched fist across chest)* Yes, sir. We don't know what to do with the Nazarene's cloak, sir. It's much too fine to tear apart.

CENT: I don't care what you do with it! Why not draw lots? Then you won't have to ruin it.

LONG: Thank you, sir. That's a good idea.

CENT: Well, get on with it. This crowd could get out of hand.

LONG: *(Saluting)* Yes, sir!

(As he leaves, the Centurion resumes his position and again looks up at the center figure. He begins to talk, as if thinking out loud.)

CENT: You've come a long way — and for what? Why didn't you stay up there in Nazareth? You must have known that only death awaited you here in Jerusalem. Surely you could have done your people more good alive than dead! What possible good can your dying on that cross do? Oh, I know what you'd say if you could hear my thoughts — "The good shepherd lays down his life for his flock." That doesn't even make sense! Your own people are the ones who put you up there. They're the ones who demanded your death. If your death is for them, from what are they delivered?

(He looks around at the mob, then back to the cross.)

You told this wretched mob — "I am the Way, follow Me." Follow you where? To this dead end — a cross? *(Pause)* I don't really understand you. You always talk in riddles. But perhaps if I think for a moment, I can remember something that you've said that can explain your being on that cross. *(Suddenly)* What am I saying? Nothing can justify such a death for you. Why, from the very first I knew there was nothing but good in you. Oh, I know Caesar had me convinced that you were a dangerous malcontent, and Pilate assured me that every evidence pointed to this fact. And I admit I began my investigation positive that I could make short work of you and your followers. But now — if Caesar knew the truth, he never would have allowed you to be —

11

NO! Caesar wouldn't lift a finger to save you! What was it he said the day he sent me here?
(Crowd noises fade and everyone "freezes." Lights on center stage begin to dim. Caesar steps out onto the elevated stage right as the lights reach blackout. The Centurion speaks into the blackout.)
I remember. He was most emphatic —
(Lights immediately come up on Caesar, and as they do, he speaks on the cue word "emphatic.")

CAES: Rome cannot allow even a whisper of rebellion to go unchallenged. Even if you find this Nazarene completely harmless, it might be well to destroy him as an example to those who might prove more dangerous!

CENT: *(Facing Caesar)* But, sir — if he is innocent of any threat to Rome, wouldn't we run the risk of creating a martyr around whom a full-scale rebellion could grow?

CAES: That's why I'm sending you — so this won't happen. I want no rebellion — no martyrs — *no mistakes!*

CENT: I understand, sir.

CAES: You have been selected for this mission on the recommendation of one of my best field commanders — Curius Messina.

CENT: I know him well, sir. I served with him in the Northern Campaign. He is an excellent officer.

CAES: He assured me that if anyone could get the job done, it would be you. Now, I want you not only to do a thorough investigation of the Nazarene malcontent, but I also want you to prove, or disprove, the rumors concerning Pilate and Herod that persist in coming to me from time to time.

CENT: Rumors, sir?

CAES: It concerns an alliance they have made with the Jews. It seems that the Jews, under the leadership of Annas, a high priest, have guaranteed peace and tranquility in the province in exchange for the right to collect taxes themselves.

CENT: That appears to be a somewhat convenient arrangement, sir.

CAES: On the surface — yes. But there's more. These Jewish tax collectors demand twice the normal tax, give the legal share to Rome, and retain the rest for themselves. I don't mind that they are clever opportunists, but this wealth is controlled by a mere handful of Jewish families. It is conceivable that this money could be used to finance a sizeable army and tempt them to rise against my legions. There is a rumor that Herod and Pilate may be foolish enough to join them. I do not believe these rumors are accurate, but —

CENT: I understand, sir.

CAES: Now, here is my plan. If you were to appear on the scene and begin asking questions, Pilate and Herod, if there is any basis to these rumors, would grow suspicious and do a thorough job

12

ot covering their tracks. So — you will enter Palestine with sealed orders for Pilate. They will contain a vague suggestion that you have been caught in some minor indiscretion in Rome, involving a youthful act of insubordination, and that perhaps a taste of frontier disciplines may help to straighten you out. I'll ask Pilate if he has any unpleasant tasks that might help in making you a better soldier.

CENT: But, sir, how is this to aid my investigation of the Nazarene malcontent? I fail to see —

CAES: *(Interrupting)* Patience, Flavius. You see, I want every move you make to appear as if it were Pilate's idea. Curius Messina, in the meantime, will send orders to Pilate inquiring if he has an officer who can look into a report that a malcontent named Jesus has been stirring up the people in the northern part of the province.

CENT: I see your plan, sir. I will be that officer, and you will have your investigation of the Nazarene —

CAES: And you will be free to ask some very pointed questions concerning Pilate and Herod.

CENT: I think it's a fine plan, sir.

CAES: Perhaps you can manage to drop a few hints now and then that you are a bit disenchanted with Caesar's treatment of you in sending you to Palistine. If Pilate is involved with a Jewish attempt at revolt, he may take you into his confidence. After all, he would certainly need a commander for his coup, and he just might urge you to join him.

CENT: Might I say, sir, that you have covered every eventuality?

CAES: It is the price one pays for power, Flavius. One must always be a step ahead of every possibility. *(Suddenly)* Oh, yes — you and Messina are the only ones, besides myself, who will know what we have talked about today. Messina will be in contact with you in Palestine through channels only he will know. When can you be ready to leave?

CENT: Within the hour, sir.

CAES: Good! May the gods go with you!

(Lights fade on this scene and immediately come up on elevated stage left. Pilate, in an angry mood, is talking to Flavius.)

PIL: And I say that you will do as I command! You will investigate this matter thoroughly. I want no zealous malcontent causing needless strife here in Palestine.

CENT: *(Faces Pilate)* But, sir — why me? I'm a soldier! I am not trained for spying.

PIL: *(Standing suddenly and pointing a finger)* And I say that you will be what I want you to be — when I want you to be! *(Sits)*

CENT: *(Pleading)* But this may take months — years. My men were

13

counting on taking part in the games. *(Getting angry)* I ask you, do you want a good showing in the games?

PIL: *(Leaping to his feet again, shouting)* Flavius! *(Pause)* You forget who and where you are! You don't ask questions! You obey orders!

CENT: *(Also shouting)* And you seem to forget that I am a centurion! I am trained for fighting — not spying. As for this malcontent — there have been dozens of these so-called saviors. And every one of them was after the same things: money — power — notoriety! I say kill him and have done with it!

PIL: No! I tell you this one is different. Kill *him* and you will have a full-fledged uprising on your hands.

CENT: *(Scathingly)* Are we Romans women — that we hide from a band of malcontents?

PIL: *(Livid)* Flavius! I am warning you. You go too far. Guard your tongue. You have your orders, and I will stomach no insubordination. *(Archly)* Or do you intend to defy me here in Palestine as you did others in Rome? Yes, I know all about your — indiscretion — in Rome!

CENT: *(After a long pause)* When do I begin, sir?

PIL: Well, now — you're playing a different tune, aren't you? Very well, here are your orders. This Nazarene has come out of nowhere. Suddenly he appeared outside our cities, preaching a philosophy of peace and humility. This doesn't fool me for one moment. He has organized a huge following. He is very smooth and, I must admit, very successful. We don't know where his funds come from, but they must be considerable. His followers give the appearance of poverty, but no one can command such allegiance unless there are ample funds.

CENT: Why not let me kill him in such a way that it will appear that his followers quarreled and assassinated him?

PIL: As I said before, we would risk having a martyr on our hands. No, my way is best. Perhaps we can lay our hands on their money, too, if we're careful. It takes money to finance such a man.

CENT: I understand, sir.

PIL: *(Pause)* Now, I want facts. If I know what I'm fighting, it will make our work much easier. Find out all you can — who finances his journeys, who his followers are. I want to know his strengths and his weaknesses. Most of all, I want to find out if he is a threat to me or to Rome.

CENT: In that order, sir?

PIL: *(Loudly)* In that order! *(Quietly again)* We do know this much. Perhaps it may help you to begin your work. Rumor has it that he was born in Bethlehem. He was a carpenter before he began organizing. Beyond that we know nothing, except that some of his followers refer to him as "Messiah." The leaders of the Temple

14

deny he is such. It might help to know that the Jewish hierarchy hates him. Maybe they know more than they've told me. Leave nothing to chance. Be thorough and waste no time. Perhaps you can complete your work in time for the games. May Jupiter guide you. Report to me when you have something of importance. You are dismissed.

CENT: Yes, sir. *(Salutes with clenched fist across chest)*

PIL: *(As Centurion turns to leave)* And Flavius —

CENT: *(Turns)* Yes, sir?

PIL: Succeed in this assignment, and I may forget your impertinence!

CENT: Yes, sir.

> *(Lights fade on Pilate as he looks after Flavius with a half-smile on his face. The crowd noises begin at the blackout and the lights come up full on center stage, with Flavius once again looking up at the cross. Soldiers are standing at attention, downstage left, in line.)*

CENT: It's very strange, Nazarene. The might of Rome was against you, and we still could find nothing to brand you a malcontent. We could find nothing to prove you a threat either to Pilate or Caesar. I do know that you are a good man and that your own people are —

WOM 1: *(Coming forward to Centurion's left, viciously)* Hey, you, on the center cross. You claim to be a king. Well — how do you like your throne?

> *(Crowd laughs)*

WOM 2: *(Taking position beside her)* Have you torn down any temples lately?

> *(Crowd laughs)*

Or perhaps you just put them back together again after someone else tears them down!

> *(Crowd laughs)*

MAN 1: *(Shouting from rear)* Hey, everyone, quiet! I think he's going to say something. Maybe he'll declare himself king!

> *(Crowd laughs, then grows quiet)*

JESUS: Father, forgive them, for they know not what they do!

> *(This voice can be spoken from backstage, through a megaphone turned toward the ceiling, or it can be spoken through a microphone at the rear of the auditorium. The voice must sound as if it comes from a man in great agony but be clearly enunciated for all to understand.)*

MAN 2: *(Derisively)* Hah! We know what we're doing, all right. You're up there because you're a fake.

> *(Crowd murmurs agreement)*

WOM 1: That's right. If you're the Son of God, come down from that cross. Then perhaps we'll believe you.

15

Wom 2: Yeah. Command those nails to just pull out of the wood while you gently float to the ground.
(Crowd laughs raucously)
Pri 1: *(Stepping forward to right of Centurion)* He said he could save others! He can't even save himself!
(Crowd roars)
Pri 2: If, as he claims, he is the king of Israel, let him now prove it to us. Come down from the cross and we will believe you!
(Crowd yells approval)
Pri 1: He trusted in God; let God deliver him now, for he said, *(Mockingly, in stentorian tones)* "I am the Son of God!"
(Crowd yells)
Wom 1: If he were God's Son, would God let us put him on a cross? I think not!
(Crowd jeers)
Man 1: *(Picking up rock)* Here — if you're a god, let's see you duck this rock! *(Draws back his hand, about to throw it)*
Cent: *(Putting out his hand angrily)* Why can't you cowards let a man die in peace? Now, get back, you jackals, or I'll have my men lay the flat of their swords to you!
Wom 1: You wouldn't dare. We have a perfect right to be here. He claimed to be what everyone knows he isn't, and that's why he's up there. *(To man with rock)* Go ahead! Throw your rock. He has no right to stop you!
Cent: *(Quietly, but with flat, menacing tone)* Perhaps you'd care to test my authority? Why don't *you* throw the rock? Hand her the rock!
Wom 1: *(Glaring at Flavius, then moving away)* Aaaahhh!
Wom 2: *(Threateningly)* Maybe Pilate would be pleased to know that one of his Roman legionnaires is protecting a condemned criminal!
Long: Hold your tongue, woman, or lose it!
(Crowd withdraws a bit, muttering to each other and glancing at the soldiers with ill-disguised venom.)
Cent: *(Looking up at cross)* She's right, you know, Nazarene. I have no right to protect you. *(Pause)* It's their right to see justice done — justice? This is justice? Not one shred of evidence was ever produced that could put you there. There's only one reason I can think of that you're hanging on that cross — political revenge. You did step on many toes! It's strange that a baby born in such humble circumstances should grow up to earn the hatred of people in high places! *(Pause)* Does it surprise you that I know where you were born? You were born in a barn. How do I know? I know a great deal about you. Your mother gave birth to you in a little stable behind an inn in Bethlehem. Oh, I've been there — and I talked to the old man who still owns the inn. That was the first

16

place I went in my investigation. After all these years, they still remembered you.

(Lights fade slowly on center stage)

But it's not so strange that they should remember — after all, many things happened that night.

(At the blackout, the lights come up on elevated stage right. Innkeeper is speaking to the Centurion.)

INN: With all the thousands of people who have stopped at my inn, you expect me to remember a family that came here over thirty years ago?

CENT: But I'm sure you will recall them. Does the name Jesus mean anything to you?

INN: Jesus? No — that's not an uncommon name, you know.

CENT: His mother was a peasant woman, quite young, and his father was a carpenter.

INN: But I seldom ask anyone's occupation.

CENT: Perhaps your wife would remember?

INN: My wife died a number of years ago — wait! My son Julian might remember. He was just a lad, but children sometimes put us older folks to shame when it comes to remembering. *(Calls offstage)* Julian! Julian! Come here! *(To centurion)* My son was only eight or nine at the time, but —

(Julian enters)

JUL: What is it, father?

INN: Julian, this officer is searching for information of someone who may have stayed at our inn over thirty years ago.

JUL: If I can help you I — *(startled)* Thirty years ago?

CENT: I know it's a great deal to ask, but perhaps you may recall them.

JUL.   Well, I was just a child, but describe them — maybe I *can* help.

CENT: It was about the time of the great tax gathering. They were both Jews. He was a carpenter — oh, yes, the young wife was very near her time with her first child. In fact, the child, a boy, was born about that time. They named him Jesus —

JUL: *(Interrupting excitedly)* Wait! Yes! I remember just such a family. They came late at night, and we had no room for them — so many people were traveling at that time. *(Turns to his father)* You remember, father — that must have been the woman who had her baby in the stable. Mother gave her the swaddling clothes.

INN: *(Suddenly)* You're right, son. Jesus — that was the name they called him. *(Turns to Flavius)* Yes, I remember it now! I sent Julian down with the swaddling clothes about the third watch.

JUL: I remember telling all my friends that we had a baby born at the inn. That night some shepherds came looking for the baby, too.

CENT: Shepherds? They came looking for this baby?

INN: That's right! They came down out of the hills from tending

17

their sheep. They told a wild tale about a sky filled with angels. They said one of the angels told them that their Messiah was born that night — and that they would find him in a stable.

CENT: What nonsense is this? Do you expect me to believe that they saw a vision and came and found it all just as the "angels" said? What do you take me for — an idiot?

INN: I don't ask you to believe anything. That's exactly what happened.

CENT: Ridiculous!

INN: Why would we lie about it?

JUL: Father, if he doesn't believe us, perhaps he would listen to one of the shepherds who was there. Isn't old Tobias still living?

CENT: You mean one of the shepherds who — *(Sarcastically)* saw a sky filled with angels? Where will I find him?

INN: Tobias lives just beyond those hills. *(Pointing to stage left)* He is very old, but his mind is still clear. I believe he still tells his story in the marketplace.

CENT: And a story for gullible children it is!

INN: Well, there were a goodly number of shepherds, and they all saw the same thing. They had no reason to lie or make up such a tale. And remember, they found exactly what they were looking for. How do you account for that? They couldn't have known about the baby. They insisted that the child was the promised Messiah.

CENT: Messiah? Did you say Messiah? That's the second time you have used that word.

INN: They not only called him Messiah, but also the King of Israel!

CENT: Some king! Born in a barn. Where did this family go after they left here?

INN: No one knows. One morning soon after they had been taken into the house across the way, they were gone. No one saw them leave. And if you're thinking of asking the people who live in that house, it won't do any good. Shortly after the soldiers came and killed their baby son, they left. No one knows where they live now.

CENT: Well — thank you for what you have told me. *(Gives them each a coin)* I'll ask the shepherd about his "sky full of angels."

JUL: Why are you, a Roman centurion, looking for this child? Is he a king, as they said?

CENT: King? There is no king but Caesar!

(The lights fade out on elevated stage right and immediately come up on elevated stage left. An aged man is seated on a bench. He is speaking to the Centurion.)

TOB: *(Speech of aged man — halting and slow)* I am Tobias the shepherd. I do not see, but I can hear the sound of your trappings. You are a soldier, aren't you?

18

CENT: I am Flavius, a centurion. I have come to ask about a story that you tell.

TOB: Ah, yes. You have come to hear about the angels. *(Quickly)* Do you mean any harm?

CENT: Not to you, old man. Why do you ask? Does the story you tell bring harm in the telling

TOB: No, Centurion. It is a tale of peace and hope.

CENT: Are you telling me that you actually believe you saw angels?

TOB: So — you already know the story?

CENT: *(Impatiently)* And you are asking me to believe such a tale?

TOB: No, my son. I ask you to believe nothing! I have told only the truth. I was there!

CENT: Perhaps the years have made the tale grow and you add an angel or two each year?

TOB: No! My story has not changed in over thirty years. Ask anyone! There were many of us in the hills that night. We all saw the same thing. It was no dream. We came and found the child — exactly as the angel said we would. Nothing can change that!

CENT: It is said that old men see many things when they gaze into a campfire! Perhaps you have gazed into many campfires over the years!

TOB: *(Struggling to his feet, straightening proudly and defiantly)* You would rob an old man of his only dignity? I tell you — my companions and I looked upon the promised King of Israel.

CENT: So — now he's a king? Could it be that you preach insurrection?

TOB: Do you think you can frighten an old man? Insurrection is for the young and strong. I know only that the angels promised us a king! By what manner he rises to the throne is in the hands of God. Now — leave me in peace!

CENT: You have no reason to fear me, old man. I only seek the truth.

TOB: Truth? Then I have further proof.

CENT: What now, old man — more dreams?

TOB: Go to the palace of Herod. There you will learn of three strangers — kings from far countries — who came seeking the same child. They came, telling of how they had followed a star. They stopped at Herod's palace to inquire the way. They finally found their way here, paid homage to the baby, left great gifts, and then went on their way. Not long after, Herod's soldiers came and slaughtered all male babies under two years of age. It was rumored that he thus hoped to kill this child who was proclaimed a king!

CENT: *(Incredulously)* Are you certain of this?

TOB: You haven't believed me up to now. Go yourself and inquire at Herod's palace. His son reigns now, but he knows of his father's fear. Perhaps you will believe your own kind. Go and see if I speak the truth!

CENT: That I shall, old man.

(Lights fade on elevated stage left and immediately come up on elevated stage right. Herod is revealed, sitting on a throne with two soldiers as guards. He is angry.)

HER: What? You come here with a story like that and expect me to believe this isn't some trick to bedevil me? You go back to Pilate and tell him that I —

CENT: This is no trick, sir! I am merely seeking the truth about this Jesus of Nazareth.

HER: Truth? Then why believe this ridiculous fantasy about three kings who never existed?

CENT: Because I know that three kings did come to this palace and that they did see your father. The whole city was in an uproar, so don't tell me there were no kings! There are witnesses! Shall I bring them in?

HER: *(Sits up straighter)* You dare to — *(Pauses, then slumps slowly and resignedly)* All right — there were three kings. I was old enough to sit in the council, so I saw and heard them. They said they were seeking the whereabouts of a king of the Jews who was rumored to be born somewhere in Judea. *(Quickly)* But that doesn't prove a thing! Whoever would claim as king someone born in a barn?

CENT: Then the old man was telling the truth!

HER: What? What old man? What truth?

CENT: *(Slowly, thoughtfully)* The aged shepherd who told me this. He claims to have seen the three kings and the child. He and his fellow shepherds were told by an angel that they would find the child lying in a manger in Bethlehem. They went as the angel directed and found the child. He spoke of the three kings also. He claims that the angel told them this child was the promised Messiah.

HER: Well, don't bother with this Jesus any longer. If he was born to be a king, his kingdom will never pay him homage!

CENT: Why do you say that?

HER: Why? Because, when those rascally kings failed to return to the palace, as they had promised, and tell my father where this so-called king was, my father ordered all Jewish male babies in Judea under two years of age to be killed. He couldn't possibly have escaped. This Jesus is an imposter, trying to capitalize on a dead baby's name. Forget him!

CENT: We have good reason to believe that the child was not killed. It is very possible that his parents escaped and returned to Galilee before your father could destroy him.

HER: *(Suddenly)* What? Did you say Galilee?

20

CENT: Yes.

HER: *(Thoughtfully, to himself)* I wonder — *(To Flavius)* I have a prisoner in my dungeon in whom you may be interested. His name is John. The Jews call him the Baptist because he calls everyone to be baptized. He claims to be some kind of messenger, sent to proclaim the coming of the Jews' Messiah.

CENT: Why should this interest me? Many have cried — Messiah!

HER: Ah, but this one is different. He claims that this Jesus whom you seek knowledge of is the Son of God! He further claims that he, John, is the one chosen of God to — how did he say it — ah, I remember. He has come to "prepare the way" for this God in human form! *(Laughs)* Imagine the Jews borrowing from our religion?! Well, John claims that he baptized this Jesus and that he is the Messaiah all Jews have been waiting for.

CENT: *(Suddenly interested)* Where does he claim this Jesus came from?

HER: Why — from Galilee. That's why I wondered if there might be a connection.

CENT: Jesus! And he comes from Galilee! And he claims to be the Messiah. *(To Herod)* May I see this — John — the Baptist?

HER: Certainly — but be careful. He's a wild one — but a smooth talker! I find him utterly fascinating. Why, he refuses to eat all the good things of life, like chicken, good red meat, and exotic dishes. He eats only dried roots, leaves, and wild honey — and drinks only water. He's peculiar, and often infuriating. And the first thoroughly honest man I have ever met! Herodias hates him — wants me to kill him. I can't say I blame her. He insulted her — and me. It seems he doesn't approve of our marriage. *(Laughs)* You want to talk to him? I dare say he'll do most of the talking! *(Turning to a guard)* Take the Centurion to see the prisoner John. See that you stay with him. I want no Roman centurion attacked in one of my dungeons! *(To Flavius)* Be on your guard, Centurion! He is a dangerous man. But he can charm you too. Be on your guard!

CENT: Thank you, sir. I believe I can manage.

(The lights fade on elevated stage right and immediately come up on elevated stage left. John the Baptist is lying on the floor of his cell, apparently asleep.)

CENT: Are you the man John, called the Baptist?

JOHN: *(Stirs and sits up slowly. He looks down upon Flavius for a moment before he answers.)* I am he. What do you want?

CENT: I come to inquire of Jesus of Nazareth. Is it true that you know him?

JOHN: Why do you ask? Are you sent by Herod to wring some new truth from me?

21

CENT: No. I am here simply to ask you about Jesus of Nazareth. It is said that you baptized him. Is this true?

JOHN: Yes, I baptized him.

CENT: Will you tell me about it?

JOHN: Why? So you can find new ways to trap and destroy him?

CFNT: If he has done no wrong, he need fear no man.

JOHN: *(Getting impatient)* That depends upon Roman interpretation of what is right and what is wrong! I lie rotting in this filthy dungeon for speaking truth! Will you twist my words and use them to persecute Jesus of Nazareth?

CENT: *(Sternly)* I twist no man's words! You need not tell me anything, but what you say may help the Nazarene.

JOHN: *(Looking searchingly at Flavius)* I believe you. You are a Roman, but I believe you!

CENT: *(Half-smiling)* I see you think little of Roman honor.

JOHN: Each man answers, ultimately, to whatever within him rules his heart — be it gluttony, sensuality, power, deceit, love, hatred, or honor. What rules your heart, Roman?

CENT: I came to ask, but you seem to be the one who seeks answers.

JOHN: *(Pause, then he smiles)* Ah, I am in the presence of a Roman who does not fear the truth and, unless the dampness of this filthy hole has warped my judgment, a man of honor. I will answer your questions.

CENT: I have learned that Jesus was born in Bethlehem and that his birth was supposed to have been announced by angels, and that three kings sought him out and paid him homage. He disappeared from sight until just recently. Now he speaks openly throughout the land. It was Herod who told me of your personal contact with him. You say you baptized him. Tell me of it.

JOHN: I was preaching in the wilderness of Judea and baptizing in the Jordan. One day Jesus of Nazareth came to me and asked that he be baptized. When he came out of the water, I saw the Spirit of God in the form of a dove descend and alight on him. Then a voice came from heaven, saying, "This is My beloved Son in whom I am well pleased."

CENT: More hallucinations!

JOHN: *(Suddenly angry)* Hallucinations! Oh, the blindness of you who perish! You Romans are the ones with hallucinations! Do you think this world is going to last forever? Do you think that Roman power is unending and invincible?

CENT: *(Sharply)* What do you know of power? Have you ever tasted cold steel? Surely you have seen the might of Rome about you. Is this all a dream that will just fade away, come some distant day? Be faithful to your hallucinations and your god in human form, but don't dismiss Rome and her might with a trite phrase!

JOHN: *(Rises slowly as he speaks)* The prophecies have been fulfilled,

Roman! *(Aroused)* The power of Rome shall melt like wax in the furnace! He shall come with all the power of the mighty God, and Rome shall vanish as the chaff blown from the winnowing floor!

CENT: *(Scoffing)* Tell me this, John the Baptist! If Jesus is the conquering Messiah, why has he left you to rot in this dungeon? Why is he any different than all the other so-called Messiahs who have crumbled before the mailed fist of Rome? Tell me, John the Baptist — where is the proof of his claim? He has never claimed to be your Messiah. Not one word has he uttered. Prove his claim!

JOHN: *(Shouting)* You Romans are blind, unbelieving fools! Where is my proof? I'll tell you. *(Speaks in quieter tone)* I sent trusted disciples to ask him if he were the promised one of Israel, or if I should look for another? His answer came back, clear and unmistakable! "Go and show John again those things which you have heard and seen. The blind receive their sight, the lame walk, the lepers are cleansed, and the deaf hear! *(Now in ecstacy of joy)* The dead are raised to life, and the poor have the Gospel preached to them!" *(Looks down at Flavius)* Look about you, Centurion! Messiah has come!

CENT: You are asking me to believe that this Jesus healed the lame — the blind — the deaf — and even cured lepers?

JOHN: And brought the dead back to life!

CENT: Either this man is a great deceiver — or he is — a — a god!

JOHN: Not A god, Centurion — but THE SON OF GOD!
(Lights on elevated stage left fade and immediately come up on center stage. The crowd sounds rise with the lights; the Centurion is looking up at the center cross.)

CENT: The Son of God? How can I believe such nonsense? The evidence to the contrary is you — hanging on that cross! The innkeeper — the old shepherd — this John the Baptist — all tried to tell me that you are the Son of God, and yet you hang there, helpless, in agony — betrayed and abandoned by your followers. *(Pause)* And yet — could you have a larger plan for men, of which this is merely the prologue? *(Suddenly)* No! In such a thought are the seeds of madness! Kill their own God — to win an ultimate victory? This is monstrous! *(Pause)* But I saw you flogged until the spark of life merely flickered, and yet no sound from you. When the nails were driven into your flesh, you uttered no groans. No mortal man could stand such pain and not cry out! *(Pause)* That's strange! All this seems related to someone with whom I spoke — not too long ago. Why should I think of that just now? I remember — it was a man called Nicodemus! What was it he said?

(Lights begin to fade on center stage. Crowd noises fade with the lights. At the blackout, the lights come up on elevated stage right, where Nicodemus speaks as the lights come up.)

NIC: No, he didn't come to see me — I went to see him. Of course, I

23

had to go at night so that no one would know that I was having discourse with him.

CENT: You had to see him in secret? Why?

NIC: It is perhaps difficult for you, a Roman, to understand these things. You see, we are the leaders of our people. We interpret the Scriptures and instruct our people in the fulfilling of the laws contained therein. I went to see Jesus secretly because I cannot allow it to be known that I associated with a man who has been responsible for instigating so much controversy regarding the interpretation of the Holy Scriptures.

CENT: You are right — I don't understand. From what I can ascertain, this Nazarene observes your every law and religious ritual. Why should there be this great gulf between you?

NIC: He is a constant source of embarrassment to the hierarchy of the Temple. He interprets the Scriptures so that every jot and tittle are observed. Then he points out that many of our traditional dogmas are embarrassingly inconsistent with the sacred intent of God's Word. His points are so well taken that many of the people are alienated from what has been the unquestioned authority for generations. If this continues, the resulting reforms are bound to create havoc throughout our faith!

CENT: Then you are opposed to him?

NIC: I didn't say that. I must confess that I consider him a man sent by God, for no man could teach or perform the miracles as he does unless this were true.

CENT: If you believe this, why do you hesitate? Believe me — if one of our Roman gods came to us in human form, we would welcome him with open arms.

NIC: But others have done mighty works before and were not Messiah. Yet the followers of Jesus claim that he is Messiah!

CENT: Then why not give him a chance to prove it? Doesn't that make sense?

NIC: But he has never claimed that title for himself. He answers all queries with riddles! We cannot decipher them.

CENT: Riddles? What kind of riddles?

NIC: For example: When I went to see him that night, I confessed to him that I felt he was sent from God; his answer was, "No one can see the Kingdom of God unless he be born again!"

CENT: Born again? You mean enter again into his mother's womb and be born again?

NIC: Those were the exact words I asked him!

CENT: Do those words mean anything to you? They are very strange.

NIC: The prophets of old spoke of such things. But it was another thing he said that puzzled me more. He said, "As Moses lifted up the serpent in the wilderness, even so must the Son of Man be lifted up; that whoever believes in him shall never die, but have eternal life."

CENT: Eternal life? Who can live forever?

NIC: In our faith, many of us believe in eternal life. I somehow got the impression that the Nazarene was telling me that he was the source of this truth. He spoke with such authority, but his words seemed filled with riddles!

CENT: You have used the word "riddles" several times. What do you mean by riddles?

NIC: That's the only way I can describe much of what he said. He appeared to be telling me spiritual truth veiled in language that was — well, almost like a riddle! For instance, one of his statements was, "For God so loved the world that he gave his only begotten Son, that whosoever believeth in him should not perish, but have everlasting life!"

CENT: (Slowly) Only begotten son? (Suddenly) Son! Now I remember! Another man to whom I spoke — not long ago — called this same Jesus the Son of God!

NIC: But that would make him equal with God! Blasphemy!

CENT: His name was John — John the Baptist. I talked to him in one of Herod's dungeons.

NIC: John the Baptist! (Thoughtfully) I remember him. He claimed to be the forerunner of Messiah — the one who should prepare the way for him! It is said that he baptized Jesus.

CENT: He told me that very thing — and I believed him. For I know men, and he was no liar. He did baptize the Nazarene.

NIC: (Slowly, with a trace of fear) Is it possible that we are opposing the Savior of Israel?

CENT: What did you say?

NIC: (As if awaking from deep thought) I was only thinking aloud. You say that John used those very words — the Son of God?

CENT: Those very words. Could it be that this Jesus is the Son — (Stops suddenly) What am I saying? A god in human form? This is ridiculous! I don't believe it!
(On his last phrase, the lights fade quickly to blackout. As Flavius repeats it in the blackout, the lights come up on center stage. Crowd noises begin. Flavius repeats the phrase a third time as he looks at center cross.)
I don't believe it! (Pause) I don't believe it!

MAN 3: (Walking up to Flavius) Don't believe what, sir?

CENT: (Startled) What? (Turns and sees man) Oh! (Pause) I was only remarking about the uncommon strength of this man here. (Points to center cross) He has stood the pain and agony without a sound.

MAN 3: (Sadly) He has helped so many to throw off their pain and hopelessness, but there is no one to help him now.

25

CENT: *(Interested)* What do you mean?

MAN 3: You are in Palestine and know nothing of the wonders he has performed?

CENT: I have heard rumors of his magical powers.

MAN 3: They are not "magical" powers, sir. He healed through faith!

CENT: Faith? Faith in what?

MAN 3: All one had to have was faith that he could heal — and it was so!

CENT: But, by what authority did he heal?

MAN 3: Our Scriptures tell us that when Messiah comes, he will show such wonders.

CENT: Then, you believe him to be your Messiah?

MAN 3: No one but Messiah could do such things!

CENT: You saw him perform miracles?

MAN 3: Saw him? I am one he cured! Once I was a cripple, but now because of him *(Indicates center cross)*, I can walk!

CENT: You were a cripple — and — *(Points also)* — he healed you?

MAN 3: Yes, it happened by the pool of —

WOM 3: Samuel!

MAN 3: Yes, mother!

WOM 3: *(Tugging at his arm)* Say nothing more. Someone may hear you!

CENT: *(Puts out his hand to stop her)* Who may hear him?

WOM 3: Please — my son talks too much!

CENT: Who are you afraid of?

WOM 3: Come, Samuel!

(They withdraw into crowd. Centurion looks up at cross.)

CENT: It's very strange, Nazarene. Where were they *(Gestures to two who have just left)* when you were being tried? All of those whom you cured? Couldn't they have helped you? If you did perform such miracles, why weren't you honored instead of crucified? For some reason, every time I question those who were healed by you, there is a strange reluctance to talk freely. They always speak as though fearful of retribution from the rulers of the Temple. It happens so often —

(Lights on center stage fade. As they do, crowd noises fade. As Flavius continues his lines, the lights black out and immediately lights come up on elevated stage left. A man and two women are there.)

I began to expect it each time I approached them! It's remarkable that I learned as much as I did.

MAN 4: You don't believe me, do you? I have said it before, and I say it again — I was blind, and now I can see!

WOM 4: Why don't you leave us alone? My brother has told you what you want to know.

CENT: But I want to know how he was cured. It is very important that I know!

WOM 4: You are in league with our leaders! You know they will excommunicate anyone who claims that Jesus is Messiah.

CENT: How many times must I tell you that I am not conspiring to betray you?

WOM 5: Then why do you ask such questions?

CENT: Because I must know the truth about this man Jesus.

WOM 5: So you can trap us!

CENT: No!

WOM 4: *(Looking at others)* Perhaps he is telling the truth. *(In a pleading manner to Flavius)* If we claim that our brother was healed in a miraculous way by this Nazarene, we will be accused of claiming him as Messiah, for these are the very things that Messiah will do when he comes. We cannot risk this.

CENT: You are actually afraid, aren't you?

WOM 4: Yes, we're afraid. You, a Roman soldier, have no fear of our religious leaders, but we don't have the power of Rome to protect us. The authorities in the Temple have commanded that we deny this Jesus, on pain of excommunication. We dare not refuse!

CENT: But this Jesus shows you fantastic miracles! You claim he heals at a word or a touch. Surely your religious leaders aren't blind to this?

WOM 5: They say he is a sinner because he heals on the Sabbath. They say that because he doesn't keep the Sabbath, he cannot be of God.

WOM 4: But some of our leaders say, "How can a sinner do such miracles?"

CENT: Your leaders can't agree on this man, and all of you stand around like sheep — doing nothing! Why don't you unite behind this Jesus and —

WOM 5: You, a Roman centurion, advocate insurrection?

CENT: I am not advocating anything. I am merely pointing out that here you have a man who does what no other man has done before, and you are actually denying him by doing nothing. Why?

MAN 4: Sir, what my sisters have not told you is that I did not deny him — and I have paid for it.

CENT: Paid for it?

MAN 4: After word had gotten around that I'd been cured of my blindness, the priests came to me and demanded that I give God the praise for my sight because this man Jesus was a sinner. I told them that I didn't know whether he was a sinner or not, but that I did know one thing — once I was blind, but now I see.

CENT: With this evidence, they must have believed that Jesus was no ordinary man.

27

WOM 4: *(Sarcastically)* Huh! *(Looking around furtively)* If you ask me, I think they're afraid of Jesus.

WOM 5: Not only that, but — tell the rest of it, Josias.

MAN 4: Well, they asked me again to describe how he cured me, and I told them I had already told them and they didn't believe — if I told it again, would they become his disciples? Then they cursed me and accused me of being Jesus' disciple and said that *they* were Moses' disciples! Then they added this — "We know that God spoke to Moses, but as for this Jesus, we don't know who he is or where he came from." At this I spoke rather hastily and made them terribly angry. *(Looks about him almost in fear)*

CENT: *(Coaxing)* Yes, yes — what did you say that made them angry?

MAN 4: I said, "This is impossible! Since the world began, no man has ever been known to have opened the eyes of one blind from birth. And now such a man performs this miracle and you, the leaders of Israel, know nothing of him!" I also added, "You know that God doesn't listen to those who are not His followers; but if a man worships Him and does His will, He listens. If Jesus, who performed this miracle, were not of God, he could not have restored my sight!" With this they accused me of being one born in sin. They said that, therefore, I had no right to teach them anything, and they excommunicated me — claiming I was a disciple of Jesus.

CENT: And are you his disciple?

MAN 4: I believe that no one but the Son of God could open the eyes of one blind from birth! *(All stand motionless and silent)*
(Lights fade slowly on elevated stage left, and at blackout lights begin to come up on center stage. Crowd noises begin and Flavius gazes at center cross.)

WOM 1: *(Comes up to Flavius, observing him gazing at cross)* What are you looking at, soldier? Are you waiting for him to come down from that cross?
(Crowd laughs loudly)

WOM 2: *(Coming forward)* Come down from a cross? No one ever comes down from a Roman cross — do they, Roman? There's a special art in the way they place the hands, just so — and the feet, just so — and then they drive the spikes in with —

CENT: Silence, woman! *(Two soldiers begin to step forward, but Flavius puts up his hand to stop them. He speaks scathingly to women.)* What manner of humans are you? You come here to gape at a dying man and make fun of his agony. These two thieves are getting their just rewards — but him? I was at his trial! Not one shred of evidence was proven against him. The words of jackals — like you — were twisted and perverted to the end that other vultures crying "Crucify him! Crucify him!" made a mockery of justice! *(Quietly)* What do you suppose would happen if he did come down from that cross? Are you so sure he won't?

WOM 2: *(Stepping back and stammering slightly as she looks up at cross)* But — our priests couldn't be wrong — he is not — the — Son of — God —

WOM 1: *(Boldly)* Of course he isn't! The Son of God hanging on a cross? Don't make me laugh!

WOM 2: *(Regaining her courage)* You're a strange one, Roman! First you crucify him, and then you defend him. I wonder what Pilate would say if —

MAN 1: *(Coming forward quickly)* Wait! The one on the left is talking to him in the center — listen!
(Crowd falls silent. A voice — labored and filled with pain — comes from the cross on the left.)

THI 1: Yes, you — in the center. You claim — to be the Christ. If this is true — why don't you show this rabble? Save yourself — and us, too —
(Crowd shifts its gaze to the other thief as he interrupts. His voice, too, is filled with pain and agony.)

THI 2: Hold your tongue! Don't you fear and tremble at what you see? If, in this hour, God is allowed to suffer, even as you and I, what awful judgment must be ours in the grave? We suffer justly, but this man is innocent of any wrongdoing! What awaits us when we face the judgment, if here on these crosses the guilty and the innocent suffer alike? Think about this before you speak again, for today you shall fall into the hands of the living God! *(Pause)* Oh, Lord, I believe you are Messiah! Have mercy on me when you come to claim your Kingdom!

JESUS: So be it. I say to you — this day you shall be with me in Paradise!

WOM 1: *(Jeering)* Hah! Paradise! He calls this paradise? Tell me, oh king of the center cross —
(Crowd laughs)
— when the vultures come down to strip the flesh from your bones, will your paradise be in the belly of a bird?
(Crowd roars raucously)

MAN 2: *(Coming forward to two women)* Quiet, you two! I think this woman is his mother.

(Mary, Jesus' mother, John, Mary Magdalene, and Mary Cleophas come on stage left. Mary Magdalene has her arm about the mother whose right arm is holding onto John's left arm. Mary Cleophas is to Mary Magdalene's left. They come slowly to center stage. Flavius steps over to stage right and watches them. As they stop below the cross, they look up. Mary raises both hands to cover her mouth, speaking these words just before hands reach her face.)

29

MARY: What have they done to you, my son?

M. MAG: *(Kindly)* I begged you not to come. Please — come away.

MARY: And leave him alone?

M. CLE: But, Mary, there is nothing you can do.

MARY: He is my son.

JOHN: We'll stay as long as you wish, Mary.

M. CLE: I'm sure my husband, Cleophas, would want me to stay with you too.

MARY: Thank you — thank you.

M. MAG: *(Looking up)* I feel so helpless. He had the power to drive the seven devils from me, but — now he refuses to use his powers to save himself.

MARY: *(Putting her hand on Magdalene's arm)* Mary Magdalene, he knew — and I knew — that if he came to Jerusalem it would cost him his life. I know it's difficult to understand, but, somehow, it is God's will that my son is fulfilling upon that cross. Don't ask me how I know — or why — I don't know the answer. That is the only thing I have to cling to — you must believe this!

JOHN: *(Gently)* Yes — he told us many times that he must come to Jerusalem and suffer great anguish, but we dared not believe him. We refused to believe him! We knew he was Messiah, but who could have possibly believed that Messiah would be nailed to a cross? *(Hopelessly)* Oh, God, is this what we have after three years of following him — a cross?

MARY: *(Consolingly)* John — John — don't give up. How do you know but that it may take a cross to fulfill God's will in our lives? We know that Gabriel did visit me; we know that angels announced his birth; we know he performed miracles — the blind see — the lame walk — lepers are healed — even the dead have come to life at his words! All this cannot have happened in vain. You must believe there is more, John — you must!

JOHN: *(Looking up at cross)* I do — I do! Only I love him so much — to see him in such agony —

M. MAG: *(Interrupting)* Mary — the Master is looking towards you. I believe he wants to say something to you.

MARY: *(Looks up at cross)* Yes, my son?

JESUS: Woman, behold your son! *(Pause)* Behold your mother!

MARY: Yes, my son — I understand.

JOHN: Master, I will take care of her. *(Turning to Mary)* Come — mother. If you won't leave, at least come back away from the crowd and rest.

MARY: All right, my son.

(The three Marys and John move to the rear of the stage and stand, looking up at the cross. As they leave, Flavius comes center, looking toward them, then turns and looks at cross.)

CENT: Then it is true? You came to Jerusalem knowing it meant your death. But why? Why are you allowing yourself to be sacrificed this way? Are you trying to prove something? Why in this hideous way? Why suffer in such agony to prove — *(Suddenly)* Wait! That must be it! You are going to perform the greatest miracle by coming down from your cross! Is that it? *(Reasoningly)* Why shouldn't you do this? With all your other miracles, you can crown your whole plan by coming down from a Roman cross. Are you surprised that I believe you did all those miracles? You needn't be. Remember — I investigated you thoroughly. I probably know more about you than any man alive. Your birth — the angels — the shepherds — the kings — the Baptist — Nicodemus — I have even talked to many whom you have healed! I believe there is something very special about you. I have a strange feeling that what you have done with your life is the beginning of something that won't end with what happens here today. Don't ask me how I know — I'm not even sure myself. But because of you, my life will never be the same! But why? *(Louder)* Why?

CAIP: *(Comes forward quickly, looking at Flavius with strange expression)* Why what, Centurion?

(Flavius starts — looks around to see who has spoken.)

CENT: I didn't speak to you.

CAIP: I'm sure you didn't. But if you weren't speaking to me, perhaps you were talking to him! *(Indicates center cross)*

CENT: *(Roughly)* And if I were?

CAIP: Isn't it rather strange behavior for the captain of a crucifixion detail to have dialogue with a condemned prisoner hanging on a cross?

CENT: *(Flatly, with hostility)* And why are you, a priest, concerned with such an oddity?

CAIP: Nicely put, Centurion. Very nicely put!

CENT: I am here because I am a soldier obeying orders. But what is so special about this crucifixion that rouses the interest of Caiaphas the High Priest?

CAIP: True — I don't usually attend such affairs. But this one concerned us in the Temple to such an extent that I felt it necessary to come.

CENT: Making sure of his death, I presume?

CAIP: *(Quickly, a bit angrily)* Your presumption is impertinent! Don't play games with me, soldier. It could prove dangerous.

CENT: *(Indicating cross)* So I see! *(Caiaphas stiffens in anger. Flavius notices that his barb has struck home and presses his advantage.)* He must have proved quite a thorn in your side!

CAIP: Guard your tongue, Centurion! *(Softens immediately)* What are we bristling over? *(Indicates center cross)* This half-dead carcass, soon to be food for the vultures?

CENT: Carcass? Food for vultures? Oh, come now — is that any way to speak of your king?

31

CAIP: Oh, yes — I was about to mention that bit of writing. I must protest, most vigorously, the wording you have used. This blasphemer is not our king! Change those words to "He said, I am the King of the Jews!"

CENT: I'll do nothing of the sort. My orders from Pilate were to put that sign up just as it is. If you want it changed, you go see him.

CAIP: That's exactly what I intend to do. You haven't heard the last of this, Centurion! *(Turns to go, but turns back for one last word)* If I were you, I would be ever so —

(He is interrupted by voice from cross. As voice is heard, they both look up.)

JESUS: My God! My God! Why hast Thou forsaken me?

CAIP: *(Triumphantly)* Now, there's something for those who followed this madman to live down. First he says he is God — and now he asks himself why he has forsaken himself! If we need any more proof that this Jesus of Nazareth is nothing but a blasphemer, there it is!

CENT: You must have a great and terrible fear of this man!

CAIP: *(Surprised)* Afraid of — of — *(Pointing)* that? What makes you think I'm afraid of him?

CENT: I'm a soldier. I have observed men under every conceivable situation. When a man fears something, or someone, that fear is always demonstrated through an unreasoning hate. When men fear an enemy, they create within themselves an overpowering hate. This makes them ready for battle. You actually fear Jesus of Nazareth!

CAIP: Ridiculous! *(Nervously looks around him)* How dare you propose such a thing. We demanded his death because he would make himself equal with God. God has commanded us to destroy anyone who blasphemes. We are merely carrying out God's judgment.

CENT: Are you telling me that your God is too weak to carry out His own judgments? I don't believe you. It may interest you to know that I was commissioned to investigate this man. I know more about him than all of you.

CAIP: Then you must know that he is an enemy of Caesar because he set himself up as a king. The very sign you put up there declares him to be a threat to Caesar. Deny it!

CENT: He was no threat to Rome. His very words exonerated him. He told Pilate that his kingdom was not of this world. If not of this world, then he is no threat to Caesar.

CAIP: Pilate must have thought so — he had him crucified! Deny that!

CENT: And I am beginning to understand that and you also! I know you for what you are.

(Caiaphas looks about helplessly, his only wish now to escape. But Flavius presses his advantage again.)

32

This man comes, fulfilling all your ancient prophecies and performing great miracles. In the very words of your Pharisees, "These miracles could only be done by someone from God!"

CAIP: I don't have to remain here and listen to this nonsense from a — a —

CENT: Why don't you say it, Caiaphas? Why don't you say "from a madman"? Isn't that the way you rid yourself of all who oppose you? *(Points to cross)* Observe your latest victim!

CAIP: You're mad! *(Turns to go, but Flavius gestures and Longinus steps up to block his way.)* Pilate shall hear of this!

CENT: I think not. You will hear what I have to say. You in the Temple fear Jesus of Nazareth because he unmasked you for what you are — power-mad egomaniacs wearing a mask of piety. Jesus has torn off your mask of hypocrisy and shown your true colors to the people who for generations have looked to you for leadership. How clever of you to turn the people against him and to use Pilate as your executioner. In one brilliant stroke you rid yourself of an opponent whom you can't stand against and establish yourselves as defenders of your faith.

CAIP: *(Fearfully)* You are not only mad, but you are suffering from hallucinations.

CENT: There's that word again! I, too, used it freely in my task of unmasking this "malcontent" called Jesus. Now I realize that I was wrong. I don't really know who of what that man is who is hanging on that cross, but this I do know — he is worth a legion of scum like you!

CAIP: *(Sputtering)* Why — you — you — Pilate shall hear of this! And your own men will be witnesses against you. *(Craftily)* You are so willing to defend this man. Perhaps you, too, are one of his followers?

CENT: *(Softly, looking at cross)* A man who could do the great things he has done? The lame walk — the blind see — the dead raised? He would be invincible! *(Louder, to Caiaphas)* If I were a follower, I would have given him my sword, my loyalty — my life!

CAIP: *(Triumphantly)* Treason! You all heard it. The man speaks treason.

CENT: I said — if I were his follower. I have no king but Caesar. But I bear more allegiance to Caesar than you do to your God! You have twisted and violated the very Scriptures you claim come from your God. The sight of you sickens me. Leave! Go to Pilate and demand that he change what he has written. Get out of my sight!

CAIP: I'll go to Pilate — and he will change that sign, I promise you. And I will also remind him that not all his soldiers are to be trusted. *(Again he turns to leave, and again Flavius gestures for Longinus to stop him.)*

CENT: You go to Pilate. I'll not stop you. But there is one thing you should know. I am here on orders from Caesar himself. I came not only to observe Jesus of Nazareth, but to look into the matter of the great tax inequities that have fattened the coffers of the hierarchy of the Temple! Perhaps you would care to challenge the personal intervention of Caesar in this matter? It might be well for you to know, also, that Caesar believes your wealth may possibly be hoarded for the purpose of financing an army to attempt to rid yourself of him. My report is somewhat in your favor, but I could be persuaded to alter a word or two, which would be sufficient to cause you and your partners — shall we say, some uncomfortable moments. The matter rests with you, Caiaphas! Now go!

CAIP: *(With controlled anger)* You may have won, Centurion, but guard your actions well from now on. I am accustomed to success in all I undertake. I speak no idle threats! *(Leaves)*

CENT: *(Calling after him)* And I shall hesitate to turn my back on you.

LONG: *(Comes up to Flavius and looks toward Caiaphas)* You have earned a most powerful enemy, sir. You will need all the influence that Caesar has to offer.

CENT: Rome has dealt with jackals like him before — and still rules the world.

LONG: He will go straight to Annas, their political advisor, and you had best be on your guard. They command the ear of Pilate and Herod as well.

CENT: My work here in Palestine is completed. Caesar will recall me at once and ask for my report. Priests will have a difficult time reaching the ear of Caesar in Rome, especially after my report is read.

LONG: *(Almost dreamily)* Rome! I have never been there. What is it like, sir?

CENT: You may have an opportunity to see for yourself, Longinus. The way you handle a short sword, you will be in great demand at the games. Would you like that?

LONG: You mean — you would take me to Rome, sir?

CENT: You need no one to take you. I have already sent word of your ability. Your orders should come through soon.

LONG: *(Standing straight with pride)* May I tell my men, sir?

CENT: Certainly.

(Longinus salutes and turns to his men. Mary Magdalene approaches Flavius.

M. MAG: Sir? How long will it be before the Master's suffering will be over?

CENT: *(Gently)* I don't know woman. Some die quickly — others may linger for hours. I've known very strong men to live for days on a cross.

M. Mag: We've tried to get his mother to leave, but she will not go.

Cent: Many mothers have stood beneath crosses on other days. They wouldn't leave either.

M. Mag: *(Hesitantly)* Perhaps if you spoke to her — tried to persuade her. She may listen to you.

Cent: But, woman — you don't understand! I gave the orders to drive the nails. I ordered the crosses raised. I am the one who crucified him! What makes you think she would listen to me?

M. Mag: You are different from the others. You wouldn't let them throw stones — and we heard you when you spoke to Caiaphas.

Cent: Well —*(Looks at cross)* This man is uncommonly strong. I fear she will have a long wait. I will speak with her.
(He starts to walk toward Mary, suddenly stops as he sees someone who is approaching from offstage.)
I must speak to this man first.

M. Mag: *(Follows Centurion's gaze)* Barabbas! *(Almost a whisper)* What is he doing here?

Cent: I'll take care of him. Return to the Nazarene's mother.
(Barabbas enters with a swagger. His entrance causes a stir among the crowd, while the priests gesture and whisper excitedly.)

Bar: *(Comes center stage to stand beside Flavius. Stands with his fists on his hips, looking up at center cross.)*
Not dead yet, eh?

Cent: What are you doing here, Barabbas?

Bar: *(Gives Flavius a casual glance)* I have a perfect right to be here. After all *(Pointing)*, this one here is taking my place, isn't he? I had to come and see how I — or he — was doing. *(Laughs)*

Cent: Not so loud. That is his mother over there.

Bar: His mother? What's she doing here?

Cent: What would any mother be doing here? Even your mother.

Bar: My mother! I don't even remember my mother — and I'm certain she wouldn't waste her time, anyway. *(Glances at priests)* Why have the priests come? Since when do the mighty princes of the Temple dirty their feet and robes at a crucifixion?

Cent: Perhaps their hatred can only be satisfied by seeing him die!

Bar: *(Indicating Jesus)* Hate him? Why should they hate him? I heard the people loved him — shouted and waved palm branches when he came to Jerusalem last week.

Cent: But it was you they chose this morning.

Bar: Bah! A paid mob chose me. What I'm interested in is why this — this — *(Looks at Flavius)* What's his name?

Cent: Jesus of Nazareth

Bar: I can't understand why this Jesus didn't defend himself. Even when Pilate offered to free one of us, he never begged or made any effort to win the mob's favor. I remember that he looked at

35

me — and that look did strange things to me. That's why I came up here to see him again.

CENT: A look brought you up here? I don't understand.

BAR: I don't understand either. All I know is that no man ever looked at me like that before. I had the strangest feeling that his look told me he — wanted to die — in my place! *(Looking up at cross)* Now, why would anyone —

CENT: He wanted to die in your place? That's ridiculous!

BAR: I know it sounds strange, but I swear that's what I felt. That's why I came up here — to — well, to see how he died.

CENT: He is a brave man. He hasn't uttered a sound of pain from the beginning. Reminds me of a sheep being slaughtered. They never struggle or make a sound either.

BAR: I have the oddest feeling. I keep thinking that I should be up there — and yet I'm not. But it's almost as if I am up there, yet I feel no pain. I swear — I feel him looking at me — just like he did at the trial. And it's almost as if he — as if he's telling me he's glad to be there in my place! But that's impossible! Why would anyone want to hang on a cross in my place?

CENT: You feel the power of this man too? I've felt it from the moment I met him. He's different from any man I have ever met.

BAR: I've heard that he is a good man — that he healed people and could perform miracles. The people say that he obeyed every letter of Jewish law. Why, then, is he hanging there? Me? I've broken every law, every tradition, every moral vow! And yet the priests wanted him dead — and used me as — as a pawn. It's the priests who put him there! They wanted him dead! But why?

CENT: I can tell you why —

JESUS: I am thirsty!

BAR: He said he is thirsty. Are you going to give him something?

CENT: *(Motions to Longinus)* Bring the sponge!

(Crowd surges forward, looking up at cross. Lights begin to dim, and a low, muttering thunder begins to grow, as from a distance. A wind is beginning to blow.)

Note: *Thunder and wind may be a sound track or created with a mechanical device. If it is possible to create the actual effect of wind blowing the clothes of the actors, it will be most effective. Thunder should grow in intensity until the lines must be shouted. Lights will dim until only one spot highlights the face of the Centurion. If this is possible, the final scene will be centered on the one character and will have tremendous impact on the audience.*

WOM 1: What happened?

MAN 1: The Nazarene called for a drink.

LONG: *(Elbowing his way forward)* Stand aside! Let me give him the sponge.

36

WOM 2: What's in it?

LONG: Vinegar and hyssop. (Holds it aloft)

WOM 2: Ugh! What awful stuff for a dying man.
(Thunder grows)

MAN 2: Look how dark the sky is getting! It's going to storm.

WOM 2: He refused the sponge. It won't be long now. I've seen others do the same thing just before they died.

WOM 1: That storm is coming fast. Which will happen first — the storm or his death?

MAN 1: I wager the storm will come in second. Look! He's in his death throes now!

LONG: (Speaks to Flavius) He can't last much longer, sir.

WOM 1: He's trying to say something. Let's see if he calls to Elias again. Maybe he thinks Elias will come and save him!
(Crowd laughs nervously.)

WOM 2: Quiet!
(Thunder crashes and rumbles.)

JESUS: It is finished!

CENT: What did he say, Longinus?

LONG: He said, "It is finished."

WOM 1: Finished? What's finished?

MAN 2: He is! (Starts to laugh, but thunder silences him.)

WOM 2: Just look at that storm!

CENT: (Looking at cross) It is finished. What do you mean, Nazarene? What is finished? Could it be that you had a purpose in all this? That you have spent your whole life for this moment? But how could you have planned it this way — unless — unless — Is it possible that this God of the Hebrews does enter men's lives? (Suddenly) What am I saying? No god would allow himself to be killed! How does one kill a god?

LONG: What is it, sir? Are you well? You have a strange look about you.

CENT: (Sternly, with some impatience) Return to your post, soldier. There is nothing wrong. (Longinus walks away, glancing back once, as Flavius again looks at cross.) What was it Nicodemus said? (Pause) "For God so loved the world, that he gave his only begotten Son —"
(Lights are all out except for dim spot on Centurion.)
I see it now! The pattern is complete! Your birth — the angels — the prophecies — your miracles — your courage and silence in the face of agony. The hatred of the priests — John the Baptist's words — "Not A god — but the Son of God" — your words to the thief — "Today you shall be with me in Paradise." (Pause) I know the answer! You are their Messiah!
(Suddenly there is silence.)

JESUS: Father, into Thy hands I commend My spirit.

37

LONG: *(Coming to Flavius, indicating Jesus)* He is dead, sir!

CROWD: *(Pressing forward)* He's dead — what did he say — what was that he said — he died too soon — did you see him die — *(And other short sentences of this type)*

(The storm crashes loudly. The crowd, soldiers, and priests fall to the ground in terror. Only the three Marys, John, and Flavius remain standing. For a long moment the storm rages, then suddenly it stops. The only light is the spot on Flavius' face. He stands looking up into the light and at the cross. Slowly he removes his helmet, kneels, and with hands extended down to his sides, he looks up at the cross.)

CENT: Surely, this man was the Son of God!

(Remains kneeling, looking at cross, as the crowd slowly rises and exits. There is no sound at all. John and the Marys remain in place, looking at cross. The soldiers stand at stage left at rigid attention. The spot begins to fade on Flavius as soon as the crowd has exited and slowly fades to blackout.)

THE VISITOR

Characters

Henry Camden — intense young student in his final year at Crestwood Theological Seminary, unshakable in his personal Christian
commitment

Dr. Phillip Thomas — Professor of Bible at Crestwood

Lucius S. Deville — Henry's visitor — rather good-looking, appears
to be in his late thirties or early forties, dressed in latest "execu-
tive-type" fashion, although he carries a cane

Paul of Tarsus — himself, a witness, dressed in long, flowing robe, he
is rather short and a bit stooped. His hair and beard are white.

Mary Magdalene — herself, a witness, attractive woman of medium
height, soft-spoken. She wears long blue robe and matching
headpiece.

Marcus Polonius — a Captain in Caesar's Imperial Army, a witness.
He is tall and powerful, dressed in trappings of a Roman soldier.

Time

The present

Place

Henry's dormitory room on the Crestwood campus

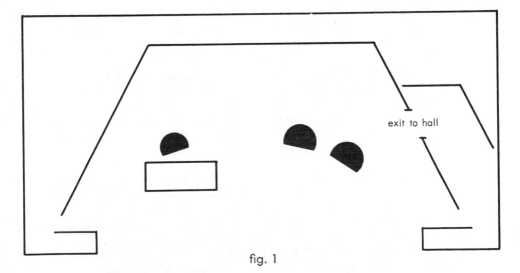

exit to hall

fig. 1

The room is a typical dormitory room. Upstage left is a single bed and night table. Centering the upstage wall is a small bookcase over which are arranged pictures, posters, pennants and such used to decorate college rooms. At stage right is an upstage door leading to a closet, while downstage is a desk (cluttered with books, papers, etc.) facing the audience, with a straight-backed chair behind it. At center stage, well upstage, are two armchairs. Downstage left is a door which opens into the hallway (see fig. 1).

(As the scene opens, Henry is seated in the center chair and Dr. Thomas is in the one to the left.)

HENRY: Then you feel I've made my approach to the subject one of cliche — and not conviction?

DR. T: Not entirely, Henry. You see, what you've done is to write about your subject with the same approach that has been used by others over and over again. I believe that you have more to offer than such stereotyped efforts.

HENRY: Stereotyped, sir? I used as my basis the four accounts of the Resurrection in Matthew, Mark, Luke, and John. Do you mean to imply that the gospels are stereotyped?

DR. T: (Laughing softly) Not at all, Henry. I mean that hundreds of students have used the same approach that you have. It is the natural reaction. Everyone sees the account through the — shall we say — eyes of the writers of the four gospels — and writes accordingly — faithfully, informatively, and intelligently. But I'm afraid a bit similar in all cases! This amounts to a somewhat stereotyped style. I truthfully expected a more original approach from you!

HENRY: (Puzzled) Original? I don't follow you, sir?

DR. T: (Patiently) I don't want to coach you, Henry — but have you ever considered how much of the evidence presented for the Resurrection would be admissable in a court of law?

HENRY: (Pointedly) But — I believe by faith, not evidence!

DR. T: I agree. But that's exactly the point I'm stressing. Everyone believes by faith. This is the foundation of our salvation. But do you realize that Jesus appeared only to those who were close to Him? Can you name any other such as Pilate — Caiaphas — the Centurion — Herod — anyone?

HENRY: Well — no!

DR. T: In fact, there is reason to believe that there is not one person who saw the risen Lord whose testimony could not be twisted, torn apart, or literally destroyed in a court of law!

HENRY: (Adamantly) I don't believe it, sir. There must be at least —

DR. T: (Quickly) Now, wait a minute! Don't tell me now. You see, you have these convictions. Prove them to me in your term paper!

HENRY: (Suddenly smiling) Trapped me again, didn't you?

40

DR. T: *(Smiling)* Not really. You *trapped* yourself.

HENRY: How many times in the past three years have you — and I repeat it — *trapped* me into doing the creative rather than the cliche?

DR. T: *(Teasingly)* Why, Henry — are you accusing me of subterfuge?

HENRY: Well — YES!

(Both laugh)

DR. T: I might add one little note of frustration. Did you know that in the account of Christ's betrayal, arrest, trial, crucifixion, and resurrection, there is but one witness whose testimony, regarding the resurrection, is the only one that cannot be disputed?

HENRY: I've never heard that before, sir. Which one is it?

DR. T: YOU tell me.

HENRY: Let's see, there's — *(He counts on his fingers, muttering the names. He gets to about ten and turns triumphantly to Dr.)* I have it! The angel who rolled the stone away!

DR. T: That's good thinking, but how are you going to get an angel into court? No, I'm afraid we'll have to rule out the angel. Not because of the difficulty of getting him into court, but because it has to be someone involved with things before the fact — *and* after the Resurrection.

HENRY: So those are the ground rules? Well — *(Begins counting on his fingers again)*

DR. T: *(Interrupting)* Why don't you put it in your paper, Henry? This is going to take a great deal of research on your part. It won't come easily, I assure you!

HENRY: *(Lowering his hands)* All right. I'll do it. But I still think there's more than one witness whose testimony cannot be disputed.

DR. T: *(Rising)* We'll see, Henry — we'll see. *(Looking at his watch)* Do you realize that it's nearly midnight? Where does the time go?

HENRY: *(Looking at his watch)* Good heavens! It *is* late!

DR. T: *(Handing papers to Henry)* Well, good luck with your term paper. *(Smiling)* I imagine you'll have it prepared by morning — you seem so confident.

HENRY: *(Laughing)* If you'll wait a few minutes, I'll hand it in now.

DR. T: I like your spirit — but doubt your productivity.

HENRY: *(Broadly)* Why, Dr. Thomas, have you no confidence in the younger generation?

DR. T: Well, my confidence is unshakable, but I know the Scriptures, and they don't just open up their treasures without a price — hard work!

HENRY: *(Raising his hands in mock surrender)* I give up! I give up! I never could win that sort of argument with you!

DR. T: You've won more than your share, I can assure you — only I never admitted it. *(Holding out his hand)* Good night, Henry. If

I know you, you'll burn a bit of midnight oil. Don't! Get some rest. A tired mind can trick one into strange conclusions.

HENRY: *(Shaking Dr.'s hand)* Good night, sir. I promise to get some rest. I need to be clear-headed to prove you wrong.

DR. T: *(Going to door)* And I might add — luck!

HENRY: And by your sly look, I'll probably need it.

DR. T: *(Laughing as Henry opens door for him)* Yes, if you insist on your preconceived notions. *(As he exits)* I'll see you in class tomorrow.

HENRY: Sure thing, sir. And thank you for giving me so much of your time.

DR. T: *(From outside)* I considered it a privilege. Good night.

HENRY: *(Standing by open door)* Good night, sir.

(Henry stands·for a long moment, looking after Dr. T. Finally he turns from the doorway, closing it slowly behind him, then walks slowly over to the desk at stage right, looking down at the papers in his hand. Reaching the desk, he is about to toss them down, when he stops, shuffles through them, and suddenly sits down at the desk to work. He looks at the door for a moment as if still seeing Dr. T. there, smiles slowly and says —)

HENRY: And I'll prove that it won't take but a few moments and surprise you in class tomorrow!

(Henry opens his Bible and leafs through the pages, jotting notes. After a few moments he leans back, rubs his eyes, then leans forward to put his head on his arms. Suddenly he straightens up.)

HENRY: What am I doing? If I put my head down, I'll fall asleep! *(Pause)* I'll just rest my eyes for a moment.

(Rests his head on his arms again. After a few moments there is a knock on the door.)

HENRY: *(Sits up with a start, looks at door sleepily. Knock is repeated. He jumps to his feet, crosses to door, speaking to himself as he walks.)*

I'll bet the professor forgot something. *(Opens door and exclaims mockingly)* The typical absent-minded professor — oh! — I beg your pardon! I thought you were Professor Thomas.

LUCIUS: *(From outside door)* I'm sorry to disappoint you, young man. I'm Lucius S. Deville. I realize the hour is late, but perhaps since you haven't gone to bed yet, we can chat a few moments.

HENRY: *(Surprised)* Why — yes — I suppose so. *(Standing aside)* Please come in, Mr. Deville.

(Lucius enters, glancing around the room briefly. As Henry closes the door, Deville crosses to center stage, turns, and faces Henry.)

LUCIUS: I imagine you are rather puzzled about my visit. Am I correct?

HENRY: *(Crossing to him)* Well — yes, a bit. *(Indicates center chair)* Won't you sit down?

LUCIUS: *(Sitting)* Thank you. I'll get right to the point. You had an interesting discussion with Dr. Thomas tonight.

HENRY: Oh! Then the professor sent you?

LUCIUS: Well, not exactly. But I did come because of your conversation.

HENRY: *(Sitting)* Then you discussed it with him and decided to come —

LUCIUS: *(Raising his hand to stop him)* No! I did *not* discuss your conversation with Dr. Thomas. I *heard* it!

HENRY: *(Surprised)* Heard it! But — I don't understand.

LUCIUS: *(Impatiently)* Oh, come now! Do I have to spell it out for you? *(Long pause, while Henry sits speechless)* You're a bright boy. But — perhaps it will help you if I confess that there is little that goes on in my kingdom that I don't know about.

HENRY: *(Still bewildered)* Your kingdom?

LUCIUS: *(Sighs audibly)* Ah, me. I thought it was just indifference. But you modern seminarians have forgotten that I exist!

HENRY: *(Sitting up rather stiffly)* I don't understand. Is this some sort of gag?

LUCIUS: Gag? I can assure you I do *not* stoop to such low humor. What do I have to do to convince you? *(Pause)* Ah! I have it. Henry — that scar on your knee. You did *not* get cut on the school grounds as you told your father. You took the shortcut through Golden's junkyard and cut yourself on the barbed wire. You were told never to enter that junkyard, weren't you? So you lied?

HENRY: But — but — how could *you* know that? I never told *anyone!*

LUCIUS: Of course you didn't. By the way, do you remember what tempted you to disobey your father?

HENRY: *(Jumps up, backs behind his chair, pointing at his visitor with look of disbelief on his face.)* Wait a minute! Are you trying to tell me that you —

LUCIUS: *(Sits back, folding his arms)* Well, now we're getting somewhere, aren't we?

HENRY: *(Points at Lucius; his lips move, but no words come out. Finally he throws his hands up in partial gesture, shakes his head, points at Lucius again and speaks in a half-laughing, disbelieving voice.)* No! *No!* I don't believe it. I must be dreaming!

LUCIUS: That's the trouble with you believers. If you can't accept anything, you call it a dream. A nightmare!

HENRY: *(Sitting down, slowly)* But — but — you don't look like — like —

LUCIUS: Ah, yes! My public image. Rather clever of me, don't you think? Dress me up in a red suit, give me a pitchfork or a spear! *(He rises, struts downstage left looking out over audience)* Better yet! Have me *sing* — all dressed up in an operatic cloak I look quite dashing — and not at all dangerous — in those settings,

43

don't I? I am rather proud of my public image. Sort of lulls the unsuspecting souls to sleep — a *long* sleep. Yes — *(Turns to Henry)* I'm rather proud of my public image!

HENRY: Now I know I'm dreaming.

LUCIUS: Why do you insist on this dream business? Go ahead — wake yourself. What is it you do? Ah, yes — pinch yourself. You believers are all alike. You preach about and shout about all the visions in that book of yours. And when you finally have a vision — all your own — you rush around bleating that *(Imitates frantic voice)* it must be a dream! Well — go ahead — pinch! All you'll get are blood blisters.

HENRY: *(Finally accepting it, he grows a bit braver.)* All right. So you're who you say you are. But tell me — what's with the name?

LUCIUS: Name? Oh, you mean Lucius S. Deville? I thought that was rather clever of me — nom de plume. It got me in the door, didn't it? After all, if I had introduced myself as "the devil" you would have thought I was some nut and slammed the door in my face!

HENRY: *(Smiling)* That's true. But has it occurred to you that I can demand that you leave now — and you would have to go?

LUCIUS: It *has* crossed my mind. But you won't.

HENRY: What makes you so sure?

LUCIUS: *(Crossing to stage right and sitting on corner of desk)* For one thing, you're dying to know why I'm here — right?

HENRY: That *has* crossed my mind.

LUCIUS: *(Smiling)* Very good, Henry Camden. Now that you've gotten over the initial shock, I think you'll probably do.

HENRY: *(Sitting up)* Do? Do what?

LUCIUS: *(Gesturing lazily)* Now, don't get all steamed up! Let me explain.

HENRY: *(Rises, walks quickly downstage left, then turns to Lucius.)* Kindly explain what you want with me!

LUCIUS: Aren't you the eager one? *(With veiled malevolence)* I'm going to enjoy this little interlude — you and your learned convictions — your ecclesiastical protestations!

HENRY: What in the world are you talking about?

LUCIUS: I'm referring to your little discussion with Dr. Thomas.

HENRY: What about it?

LUCIUS: You're so sure of what you claim to be a firm theological stand! I'm referring to your claim that there is literally a *host* of witnesses to the Resurrection.

HENRY: Ah-h-h! Now I understand. That kinda shook you up, heh?

LUCIUS: Shook me up? Oh, come now — I've been laughing ever since you made that ridiculous statement. Believe me, you couldn't be more wrong.

HENRY: *(Confidently)* Wrong? Then why did you bother coming?

44

LUCIUS: That was a good answer! Perhaps you may offer a stimulating encounter. All right. You want to know why I came? I'll tell you. I've had my eye on you for a long time.

HENRY: I'm terribly flattered. But why me?

LUCIUS: Oh, I don't know really. Perhaps it's because you think you know so much about what happened 2,000 years ago. Or — maybe it's because you think you can change this world of mine. You realize, of course, that this *is my kingdom.* Have you forgotten that? Remember, it was mine to offer — as I did in the wilderness?

HENRY: I remember. I also recall that you took a sound thrashing at that time, too!

LUCIUS: *(With a wave of his hand)* Huh! I lost a mere skirmish. Unimportant!

HENRY: *(Pointedly)* It seems you've lost a great many — skirmishes.

LUCIUS: So? Win a few — lose a few. That's life!

HENRY: All right. You haven't come here to discuss wins and losses. Why don't you get to the point?

LUCIUS: A good idea. Now — *(He crosses to Henry)* you made the claim that you could find any number of witnesses to testify to the Resurrection. I say that I can dispute, successfully, any witness you have to offer.

HENRY: *Any* witness?

LUCIUS: Any witness. You name them, I'll discredit them. *(Quickly)* Mind you — the rules governing a court of law apply!

HENRY: I was *about* to question your ground rules. What are they?

LUCIUS: *(Crosses downstage left)* I'll make it easy for you. *(Turns and faces Henry who has moved to center stage)* If you don't like any of my ground rules, we'll eliminate them!

HENRY: That's magnanimous of you. But I don't think that will be necessary.

LUCIUS: Aren't you the confident one! All right! Here they are. You may call any witness you wish.

HENRY: *(Turns to face Lucius)* Wait a moment! Call any witness? That's unfair! All my friends are sleeping. I'd have precious few witnesses.

LUCIUS: Who said anything about your friends? I'm speaking of *anyone* — even if they lived 2,000 years ago or more!

HENRY: *(Bewildered)* T — T — Two thousand years ago? You mean bring them *here?*

LUCIUS: Surely you don't think I would expect you to question witnesses if they weren't here? You name them, I'll produce them! I'll include anyone who ever lived: prince, king, commoner — rich, poor, famous, or infamous! You name them, I'll produce them!

HENRY: *(Incredulously)* You mean here — in this room?

LUCIUS: *(Gaily)* Why, of course! What did you think I meant? You call them, and I'll see to it that they come right in that door!

45

Now — are you satisfied? Any more questions?

HENRY: *(Amazed)* No — No! *(Softly)* What are your other rules?

LUCIUS: *(Crosses to Henry)* Very simple. No angels and no one of the Trinity. Agreed?

HENRY: *(Still somewhat dismayed, speaking almost as in a trance)* Agreed.

LUCIUS: You interrogate your witness, and I'll have the right to cross-examine. *(Raising a hand)* Oh, yes — one more thing. So that there will be no unqualified or unsubstantiated claims *(He indicates audience)*, we shall allow a portion of humanity to watch and listen. We will let them be our judge and jury — sort of help in keeping the record straight.

HENRY: Look who's talking about "Keeping the record straight!"

LUCIUS: *(Rather testily)* I should advise you against slurs and innuendos!

HENRY: *(Smiling)* Touched a bit of a sore spot did I?

LUCIUS: Not at all. Remember, I'm a "pro" at such tactics. I just don't want anyone to think I took advantage of your — ah — immaturity and inexperience!

HENRY: *(Smoothly)* Your concern touches me deeply!

LUCIUS: *(Equally as smooth)* I *thought* you'd appreciate my gentler side. Shall we get on with it?

HENRY: Right! *(Suddenly)* Ah — don't you think we both ought to make our opening remarks? Sort of state our cases briefly?

LUCIUS: *(Wearily)* Oh, all right! I assure you, you will look awfully silly! But — *(Lucius bows, with exaggerated politeness, smiles, and gestures for Henry to "take the stage.")*

HENRY: *(Coming downstage and speaking to the audience)* Ladies and gentlemen of the world . . .

LUCIUS: *(Snorts derisively and walks upstage)*

HENRY: *(Pauses and looks briefly at Lucius)* Ladies and gentlemen of the world! I propose to prove, beyond the shadow of a doubt, that witnesses, regarding the Resurrection, are not only numerous, but also unimpeachable! Thank you!

(Henry turns, bows to Lucius, indicates the audience is his, and walks upstage left)

LUCIUS: *(Slowly walks downstage center, pauses and looks over audience for a moment dramatically.)* Huh! *(Turns back to Henry)* Call your first witness. *(Crosses left to desk and sits on the corner of it.)*

HENRY: *(Crossing down left)* I call my first witness, the greatest witness for Christ the world has ever known.

LUCIUS: *(Sarcastically)* We can dispense with the editorializing. Whom do you call?

HENRY: I call Paul of Tarsus.

LUCIUS: I might have known. Very well — *(In a stentorian tone)* Paul of Tarsus, stand forth!

(There is the sound of distant thunder, and Paul enters from stage left. He walks slowly to center stage and looks about him with actions befitting an old man. His eyes finally light on Henry.)

PAUL: Why have I been called from my rest? *(He looks about)* And what strange place is this? *(Looks again at Henry)* I do not recognize your dress. What country are you from, and why have I been brought here?

LUCIUS: *(From stage left)* You have been called to testify to a fable. May I present Henry Camden?

PAUL: *(A bit startled by Lucius' voice. Turns to him, pauses a moment, then points at him.)* You — I recognize you by your voice. You are the great blasphemer! *(Turning to Henry)* But why is one so young — and with such a good face — in such company?

HENRY: *(A bit cautiously)* Are you really Paul of Tarsus?

PAUL: Yes, my son, I am. *(Quickly glancing from one to another)* Ah, now I see! This great perverter of the truth has come to you and challenged you! *(To Henry)* How may I serve you, my son?

HENRY: I wish to ask you certain questions regarding the resurrection of Jesus Christ.

PAUL: So? What do you wish to know?

HENRY: First, did you, or did you not, see with your own eyes the risen Savior?

PAUL: I did.

HENRY: *(Glancing in triumph toward Lucius and then back to Paul.)* And there were others with you at the time who shared your experience?

PAUL: Yes, there were a goodly number. It was best to travel in large numbers for protection. Thieves and robbers roamed the countryside. And, of course, I was accompanied by many assistants in my work.

HENRY: Then they were also witnesses to your meeting with Jesus Christ, the risen Savior?

PAUL: Yes.

HENRY: Would you describe exactly what happened?

PAUL: Gladly. *(Somewhat apologetically)* Young man, do you mind if I sit down? I am somewhat weary!

HENRY: *(Quickly)* Not at all, sir! *(Offers him the chair at center stage. Paul sits.)*

PAUL: I was on my way to Damascus, accompanied by those who were to help me ferret out all who claimed Christ as the Son of God. At approximately noon, a terribly bright light shone above us, brighter than the sun! My companions and I fell to the ground. Then I heard a voice calling my name! "Saul! Saul! Why do you persecute me?" I looked up into the light and I saw Him!

47

HENRY: Whom did you see?

PAUL: I saw Him whom I know to be the risen Savior. I didn't recognize Him at first, so I asked, "Who are you, Lord?" And He answered me, "I am Jesus whom you are persecuting!" Suddenly I was filled with a great fear and I trembled! I knew that I could not defend myself against such great power. I asked, "What do you want me to do, Lord?" He answered, "Go into the city, and I shall reveal to you what I want you to do!" Then the light faded away. I could no longer see Him. Suddenly I discovered a terrible thing — I was blind! As soon as my companions saw my condition, they took me into the city and cared for me in the home of Judas, a dear friend. *(Pause)* Shall I go on, or have I told you what you must know?

HENRY: It is enough, sir. You are certain that the one whom you saw was the risen Savior?

PAUL: I have no doubt!

HENRY: *(Turning to Lucius)* Your witness. Discredit his testimony if you can!

LUCIUS: *(Glances at Henry, crosses to Paul, stopping just to his right.)* Well, we meet again. I trust you have been well?

PAUL: *(Looking straight ahead, speaks with pointed politness)* Shall we dispense with the amenities and get to your point — which, I have no doubt, will be revealing!

LUCIUS: *(Patronizingly)* Oh, come now, Paul of Tarsus. Do I sense a note of misgiving in your voice? At least you have your feet on the ground, which is more than I can say for your young friend here! I might add, your poor, deluded, *and defenseless,* young friend!

PAUL: Aren't you counting the harvest before the reaping? You haven't forgotten Job, have you?

LUCIUS: Job was just a skirmish. Let me remind you of my many victories!

PAUL: *(Impatiently)* You are wasting time! Do what you must and allow me to return from whence I came.

LUCIUS: Very well! *(Suddenly all business)* Paul of Tarsus, I agree that you and your companions did see a great light. But, tell me again — what time of day was it?

PAUL: You know very well it was about midday!

LUCIUS: *(Sarcastically)* Don't tell me what I know! Just answer the questions please! So — it was high noon. You say the sun was shining brightly?

PAUL: Yes.

LUCIUS: And you say a *voice* spoke to you?

PAUL: Yes. It was the voice of —

LUCIUS: *(Quickly interrupting)* Just answer the question.

PAUL: *(Getting a bit angry)* Now, wait a minute! I am not on trial here! You are acting as if this were a court of law, a trial!

LUCIUS: Oh, come now, Paul of Tarsus. The next thing you will be claiming is Roman citizenship! Don't be difficult. *(In a weary manner)* After all, we have our *ground* rules here! This is the twentieth century, and you have been *resting* for 2,000 years. Now, just answer the questions, and you may return to your rest. *(Paul relaxes slowly. Lucius continues)* Now, where was I? Oh, yes! You were about to say that you heard someone's voice! Well, you may or may not have heard a voice. You might even have seen someone. I'll not dispute that. But what I want to know is, did anyone *else* see, or hear, this — this — this apparition?

PAUL: It was no apparition, as you call it. It was —

LUCIUS: *(Again interrupting)* Just answer the question!

PAUL: *(Frustrated)* Yes.

LUCIUS: You're quite sure?

PAUL: Yes, I'm sure!

LUCIUS: Now we're getting somewhere. Just whom — or what — did they see?

PAUL: Even as I, they saw a great, brilliant flash of light. And then heard the voice speaking! *(In awe)* Then, there He was!

LUCIUS: *(Quickly)* Stop right there! *They* saw a great light?

PAUL: Yes.

LUCIUS: Possibly a flash of lightning, wouldn't you say?

PAUL: No! There were no storms threatening.

LUCIUS: Perhaps it was a meteorite.

PAUL: *(His voice rising)* I tell you it was none of these. It was a supernatural light!

LUCIUS: *(Still confident and suave)* I know you are a man of great and far-reaching wisdom, Paul of Tarsus, but are you, with all your other talents, claiming to be an expert meteorologist too? What makes you so certain it wasn't a meteorite?

PAUL: It takes no great wisdom to distinguish a natural phenomenon of nature from a supernatural happening!

LUCIUS: I agree. It takes no special wisdom — only a head exposed to the hot, searing, midday sun.

PAUL: If you are hinting that I was affected by the midday sun and heat, you are wrong!

LUCIUS: Am I? Let us consider the facts, not fantasy. *(Deliberately counting on his fingers)* One, it was a hot, clear day. Two, it was midday, when the sun was at its hottest. Three, you fell to the ground, and when you could stand again, you were blinded! *(Pause)* Could it be that you saw an hallucination during the time that you were stricken by the sun and heat? In your delirium you looked full into the sun and, naturally, your eyes were affected — even for days!

PAUL: *(Insistent)* You forget that my companions were affected also.

LUCIUS: *(Smoothly, as he crosses behind desk to stage right)* Ah, yes, your companions. They also were thrown to the ground. They also saw a brilliant light. They heard a sound. Very simply explained. You were probably nearing Damascus. Perhaps the sun reflected off the spire of a gilded parapet or tower, full in your faces. At this precise moment, there occurred a common phenomenon of nature in that area. *(Lucius suddenly leans forward with hands resting on left edge of desk. His whole attitude is one of a trial lawyer as he vigorously presses his points home!)* An earthquake! Naturally, you were all thrown to the ground. You were affected the most because of a mild sunstroke. You looked up into the sun and imagined you saw and heard someone!

PAUL: *(Looking at Lucius and saying firmly)* No!

LUCIUS: *(Pressing his point even more vigorously!)* By your *own* account of the incident, you ascertain that the men with you saw *no one!* They only heard a *sound!* It was merely the rumble of the earthquake! *(Loudly)* Isn't that *right*, Paul of Tarsus?

PAUL: *(There is a moment of frozen silence. Lucius leans forward over the desk. Paul looks at him. Henry is still.)* *(Quietly)* No matter what I would say, you would twist it into one of your lies. I tell you I saw the risen Savior and He spoke to me! All your scheming and all your twisting of the truth cannot change that! *(Pointing at Lucius)* You know the truth — and I know the truth! *(Pointing at Henry)* And before this night is over, he will know the truth!

LUCIUS: *(Still leaning forward, hands resting on desk, smoothly)* Very courageous words. The fact still remains — what you have said has not changed a thing! *You* are the only one who saw anyone! *You* are the only one who heard any voice! *You* are the only one who was blinded! Even your companions who were right there cannot substantiate any but the most ordinary of happenings! You have not proven the Resurrection by your testimony! You are dismissed! *(Lucius sits quickly in chair behind desk)*

PAUL: *(Rises slowly and crosses left to Henry)* My son, I don't know why all this is happening, but I know that all things work together for good to those who serve Christ's Kingdom. Remember this well — you are sent to preach the good news of His resurrection, not to prove it. Keep in mind that the preaching of the Cross of Christ is foolishness to them that perish. But to us, who are saved, it is the power of God! *(Paul briefly looks into Henry's face, turns, and exits slowly. Henry watches him go.)*

LUCIUS: *(After Paul has gone)* Well, Henry Camden, perhaps you have second thoughts after all. Your greatest preacher didn't help your cause, did he?

HENRY: *(Turning and crossing to center stage)* Do you hate him so much that you had to bully him like that?

LUCIUS: *(Holding out his hands)* Hate him? My boy, you have it all wrong! I *admire* him greatly — and he respects me. It can never be said of Paul of Tarsus that he ever underestimated me as an opponent! But let's face it — your position is untenable! You saw how easily my points prevailed!

HENRY: I could have touched upon his miraculous conversion. *That* you could not dispute.

LUCIUS: Perhaps not, but that still would not have shown any *proof* of a resurrection. In a court of law, the fact that he shifted allegiance could easily be used to refute his testimony! So, you see, even *that* could be used against him.

HENRY: You think of everything, don't you?

LUCIUS: *(Sitting down and putting his feet up on the desk top)* I'm not known as a gracious loser. And I intend to win this little skirmish!

HENRY: *(Crossing downstage left)* Well, you'll have a difficult time discrediting my next witness.

LUCIUS: We shall see. Whom do you call now?

HENRY: Mary Magdalene!

LUCIUS: Very well! *(Rises and crosses to just left of desk. He calls as before.)* Mary of Magdala, stand forth! *(There is the sound of distant thunder. Mary Magdalene enters and stands left-center stage. She looks about questioningly.)*

MARY: *(Bewildered)* What place is this? *(Noticing Lucius)* Who are you? Your dress and this room are so strange!

LUCIUS: Welcome to the twentieth century, Mary Magdalene.

MARY: *(Looking at him questioningly)* You know me?

LUCIUS: *(Acting surprised)* Why, Mary! Has it been so long?

MARY: *(Suddenly recognizing him, she takes a short backward step and exclaims in a hoarse whisper.)* YOU!

LUCIUS: *(Mocking her with a slight bow)* Ah! Then you *haven't* forgotten!

MARY: *(Composing herself)* Leave me! You have no power over me!

LUCIUS: *(Raising a hand in admonition)* Only the power to tempt you — *and* to summon you here. *(Reassuringly)* But this is — well — sort of a social call, shall we say! My young friend here would ask a question or two of you.

MARY: *(Turning to Henry)* Young friend? *(Indicating Lucius)* He calls you his — friend?

HENRY: *(Realizing her train of thought)* It's not what you think, Miss! You see, I have — I mean, we have —

LUCIUS: *(Breaking in. He sits on desk again as he begins to speak.)* What he is trying to say is, we are conducting a survey. A sort of contest, if you will!

51

HENRY: Let's not beat around the bush, Deville! Why don't you just tell her the truth? Or is that *stretching* your powers a bit?

LUCIUS: *(Ignoring the barb)* The truth? Aren't you a bit wary of the truth, seeing how it served your friend Paul?

MARY: *(Quickly)* Are you a friend of Paul?

LUCIUS: *(Laughing)* Friends? They're more like *two of a kind! (More laughter)*

MARY: *(To Henry, in a puzzled manner)* What does he mean?

HENRY: It's only his warped sense of humor. Let me explain. I only know Paul through his writings in the New Testament.

MARY: New Testament? What is this New Testament?

LUCIUS: *(Still laughing)* It's a fairy tale written by dreamers!

HENRY: *(Patiently)* Mary, Matthew and Mark and Luke and John all wrote biographies of Jesus' life here on earth. These biographies and letters, all written under the direction of the Holy Spirit, have been preserved and put into books. We call this collection the "New Testament." By it, we have learned of Jesus Christ and that He is the Son of God, that He came to earth to die for us, that He arose the third day, and that all who believe this are saved and shall have eternal life. It tells all about Paul and Peter and John; in fact, about all who knew and loved Jesus. It tells all about you, too, Mary.

MARY: *(Softly)* It tells everything about me?

HENRY: Well, not everything, Mary, but enough to let us know that you were a wonderful and very special person!

LUCIUS: *(Impatiently)* Come, come, come! What has this to do with her testimony? I haven't all night, you know!

HENRY: *(Ignoring the outburst)* For nearly 2,000 years the truth of the Resurrection has been preserved so that all men may learn and believe.

MARY: *(Softly)* You mean, you never saw Jesus—and yet you believe?

HENRY: Yes, Mary — I believe.

MARY: *(She looks steadily at Henry for a long moment)* What do you wish to know?

HENRY: *(Indicating Lucius)* He declares that no one's testimony as to proof of Christ's resurrection can stand up in a court of law. I say it can. Through his powers, he is calling anyone I wish to interrogate on the matter. That is why you're here.

MARY: *(Defiantly)* I saw the risen Lord! My testimony is true! It cannot be disputed!

LUCIUS: *(Sarcastically)* Are you sure, Mary of Magdala?

HENRY: *(Quickly)* Wait a minute! I claim the right of questioning the witness first!

LUCIUS: *(Bowing deeply)* I beg your pardon! Proceed.

HENRY: *(Turning to Mary)* Mary *(indicates center chair)* please sit

52

down. *(Henry waits until she's seated)* The Scriptures tell us that Jesus appeared to you in the garden. Is this true?

MARY: Yes! It is true!

HENRY: He spoke to you. Is *this* true?

MARY: Yes!

HENRY: Is it true that you also saw two angels in the tomb?

MARY: Yes!

HENRY: Did they speak to you?

MARY: Yes! They asked me why I was weeping, and I said it was because they had taken away my Lord and I did not know where they had laid Him!

HENRY: Then what did you do?

MARY: Someone behind me also asked why I was weeping and who it was I sought. I thought it was the gardener and asked him where Jesus' body was. Then this person said, "Mary!" I turned around — and it was Jesus!

HENRY: Jesus — alive! *(Turning to Lucius)* Your witness! I'm sure you can't accuse her of having sunstroke!

LUCIUS: *(Smiling)* I'm afraid not. It *was* rather early in the day for such an accident. Mary of Magdala, you have stated that Jesus appeared to you at the tomb. Is this true?

MARY: Yes!

LUCIUS: Very interesting! Tell me — don't you think it rather strange that He appeared to you alone? Why didn't He show Himself when the other women were there? Why not when Peter and John were there? How do you answer this, Mary of Magdala.

MARY: I cannot answer that. All I know is that He chose to appear to me at that time. As for the other women — He *did* appear to them as they went to find the disciples, after they, too, had seen the two angels in the tomb!

LUCIUS: *(As if remembering)* Ah, yes, the other two women. Let's see — that must have been Mary, the mother of James, and Salome — right?

MARY: That is true.

LUCIUS: Now, perhaps we can shed a little light on this! Is it true, Mary of Magdala, that you were, at one time, possessed of not one, but *seven* devils?

MARY: *(Quickly)* You know it's true! Jesus cast them out of me!

LUCIUS: Oh? *Jesus* told them to get out of you. *(Snaps his fingers)* Just like that?

MARY: If you mean, He commanded them to leave, yes!

LUCIUS: *(Thoughtfully)* I see. *(After a pause)* Tell me, did you have any recurrences of the devils?

MARY: *(Firmly)* No! If you are suggesting that a devil caused me to see an apparition —

53

LUCIUS: I never intimated any such thing — but you have! So, there must have been some doubt in your mind, true?

MARY: No! It was no apparition or vision! I tell you it was the risen Lord! *(Getting excited)* I saw my risen Lord!

LUCIUS: *(Pointedly)* *Your* risen Lord? You speak the truth, Mary of Magdala! He's all yours, because this risen *Lord,* as you call Him, was solely the figment of *your* unstable mind! Your grief at losing a true and valued friend caused you to create this imaginary *Risen Lord!* Admit it!

MARY: *(Loudly and with great emotion)* You're twisting my words! You make it sound as if I were the victim of a mental disorder — but it's not true! Jesus is alive He walked out of that tomb!

LUCIUS: Did you see Him walk out of the tomb?

MARY: No, I didn't actually see Him walk out. But I saw Him walking in the garden! He spoke to me! *(Suddenly remembering)* And Mary and Salome saw Him, too. You can't say that they were victims of a devil!

LUCIUS: No, I don't believe they were. But they could have said they had seen *your* risen Lord to humor you and save you from any-more grief!

MARY: *(Calmly and with great restraint)* Jesus warned us about you! He called you the great deceiver — the great liar. How right He was! You can't bear the truth, so you twist and pervert it with lies and half-truths!

LUCIUS: I speak only from the facts laid before us! Show me where I have lied. Your testimony is of such doubtful origin that it cannot withstand the simplest cross-examination! It is unsubstantiated and completely discredited! Mary of Magdala — you are dis-missed!

MARY: *(Turning to Henry before she leaves)* I am truly sorry, sir! He knows my testimony is true, but he twists everything to suit his lies! I can only say that you *have* the words of truth, and I am sure you will be victorious! God bless you!

(Mary walks slowly out the door; Henry looks after her.)

HENRY: *(Gently)* Thank you, Mary Magdalene.

LUCIUS: *(Sarcastically)* Are you convinced, my eager young friend?

HENRY: *(Turning to him angrily)* Don't call me your friend! Don't use that word again!

LUCIUS: *(Unperturbed)* My, my! Temper! Temper! Are you going to use that in place of reasoning? It won't work fr — er — my learned opponent. Why not call it a day.

HENRY: *(Crossing downstage left and controlling his anger)* You'd like that, wouldn't you? You'd like me to just — give up — in my anger, command you to leave, wouldn't you? Well, I'll not give you that satisfaction! If you recall, Dr. Thomas assured me that there is at least one witness you can't refute, and I'll find that one, *you* may rest assured, should it take the rest of the night, or a thousand nights!

LUCIUS: *(Taunting him)* My! We *are* getting desperate, aren't we? What became of that *host* of witnesses you were going to produce? *(Lucius throws back his head and laughs)*

HENRY: *(Testily)* Shall we get on with it?

LUCIUS: *(Magnanimously)* Oh, by *all* means, let's get on with it! Who is your next victim — I beg your pardon! Your next witness?

HENRY: One I'm certain you will have a difficult time discrediting!

LUCIUS: We shall see! Whom do you wish me to summon?

HENRY: One of the soldiers who guarded the tomb.

LUCIUS: *(Startled)* What? One of the sold — Oh, come now! I couldn't have heard you ask for one of those bewildered, bewitched, and befuddled clowns!

HENRY: You heard me! *(Quickly)* Or is there a reason you're stalling?

LUCIUS: Stalling? Be realistic! One of the soldiers? They were asleep. How can they —

HENRY: *(Knowingly)* Why are you so insistent? Could it be that you fear the testimony of one who was there at the Resurrection?

LUCIUS: Afraid? Hah! I'm just amazed that you should try to use the testimony of a Roman soldier! A pagan! Are you *that* desperate?

HENRY: Are you trying to run my interrogation?

LUCIUS: *(Raising his arms in resignation)* All right! All right! I was only trying to save some time! You may have your Roman soldier! *(He turns to the door)* Soldier of Rome, stand forth!

(There is again the sound of distant thunder, and a Roman soldier enters. He looks about him in evident bewilderment. Upon seeing Henry and Lucius, he snaps stiffly to attention, saluting with a clenched fist across his chest, then stands perfectly still.)

SOLDIER: Marcus Polonius, Captain in Caesar's Imperial Army, reporting.

LUCIUS: At ease, Captain.

SOLDIER: *(Relaxing, spreads feet apart and clasps hands behind back)* Thank you, sir! *(Looking about)* What place is this?

LUCIUS: This is the twentieth century, Captain. This young man wishes to question you on a very serious matter.

SOLDIER: *(Dropping his hands to his side and bringing his feet together in great surprise)* The twentieth what?

HENRY: Don't try to figure it out, Captain. Even I am not so sure it isn't all a dream!

SOLDIER: *(Turning to Henry, looking him over)* What province are you from, sir? I have never seen clothes such as you have before!

LUCIUS: *(Breaking in)* Captain, you are here to answer questions! Will you be so kind as to speak only when asked to?

SOLDIER: *(Stiffening a bit and taking a step toward Lucius, reaching for his sword)* No one speaks to Caesar's legionnaire in such tones!

LUCIUS: *(Putting up his hands, palms facing the soldier)* Steady, man! You have no quarrel with me! *(Indicates Henry)* He has ordered you here. I am but his faithful servant! *(He bows)*

SOLDIER: *(Belligerently turning back to Henry)* And what do *you* want with me?

HENRY: I wish to question you about the tomb of Jesus of Nazareth.

SOLDIER: *(Resignedly)* Oh, not that again!

HENRY: Why do you say that?

SOLDIER: I have told that story a hundred times! *(Waving his right arm)* I do not wish to speak of it anymore!

HENRY: *(Gently)* A great deal depends on what you tell me, Captain! Won't you please answer a few questions?

SOLDIER: *(Looking back and forth from Lucius to Henry, finally to Henry)* You at least speak with a civil tongue. *(Indicating Lucius)* He speaks as if he owns me!

LUCIUS: W-e-l-l ?

SOLDIER: *(Snapping to attention)* I belong to Caesar! I owe him my allegiance, my sword, my life.

LUCIUS: *(Scathingly)* And who owns your soul?

SOLDIER: *(Quickly)* *No* man claims *my* soul!

LUCIUS: Hah!

SOLDIER: *(He again lays his hand on his sword and takes a step toward Lucius.)* *No* man calls *me* a *liar!*

LUCIUS: *(Suddenly standing tall and pointing a finger at him, Lucius speaks menacingly and with firm authority. At the gesture, the solider stops in mid-stride and freezes.)* That's the second time you have threatened to bare your sword to me! I'll not afford you that luxury a third time! Now! I ask you once more! *Who* owns your soul?

SOLDIER: *Slowly his belligerent attitude melts away. He moves back a step or two, hesitatingly lifts his right hand, points at Lucius and whispers hoarsely. Not so much an answer, as an exclamation signifying his recognition as to who Lucius really is)* You!!

LUCIUS: *(Setting back)* Now that *that* little matter is understood, shall we continue? You may do what he asks *(Indicating Henry)*.

SOLDIER: *(Looking transfixedly at Lucius, he finally tears his eyes from him and slowly turns to Henry)* What do you wish to know?

HENRY: You were the captain in charge of the watch that was set over the tomb of Jesus of Nazareth?

SOLDIER: I was!

HENRY: Were you there the morning of the third day?

SOLDIER: Yes! We had been ordered to set up our tents in the garden where the tomb was. In fact, we were ordered to seal the tomb

56

and remain there on guard. We were not to leave the area for any reason! I don't mind telling you, it was a weird place. Nothing but tombs and strange sounds!

HENRY: Would you please tell us what happened on that third morning?

SOLDIER: *(Beginning almost as if in a dream)* Well, it was about dawn. I was standing the morning watch. Just as the sun began to come up, I —

(Lucius is suddenly stricken with what appears to be a fit of coughing. The soldier stops in mid-sentence and, as if awaking from a trance, looks at Lucius. He suddenly snaps his finger and turns to Henry.)

Oh, did you say the morning of the *third* day? I'm sorry. I began to tell you of the *second* morning! Well, the morning of the *third* day *(seeming to suddenly remember)* oh, yes! That was the morning when we all —

HENRY: *(Suddenly he interrupts.)* Wait a minute! *(He turns to Lucius.)* Are you coaching the witness?

LUCIUS: *(All innocence)* Who, me? Me coach *your* witness? *(Quickly he seems to remember)* Oh, you think the coughing was meant as some sort of signal!

HENRY: I don't *think* it was; I *know* it was!

LUCIUS: *(Serious)* How can you say such a thing? We'll ask the witness! *(Turning to the soldier)* My good man, have I coached you in any way whatsoever?

SOLDIER: *(Innocently)* Why no, sir! No sir!

LUCIUS: *(Spreading out his hands to Henry)* There — you see? How can you even *imagine* such a thing?

HENRY: *(Keeping his eyes on Lucius, but talking to the soldier)* You are not to be influenced or threatened by this man! Now continue. What happened on that third morning?

SOLDIER: Well, it was quite ridiculous, sir. We had been there for three days and had been standing constant watch. You can understand, sir — four hours on and four hours off. After a while one gets very tired and — and — well, bored! I really couldn't blame my men. And I'll admit, I was pretty tired too! Well, to make a long story short, we all fell asleep! And *(Slight laugh)* while we were sleeping, those sly, sneaky disciples came and stole the body of Jesus of Nazareth — slick as a peeled willow wand. Clean away, sir! It was pretty embarrassing. You know — Roman soldiers — and me being an Imperial Captain and all! Lucky for us our commander was really understanding, and —

HENRY: *(Very angry)* All right! You can stop the playacting, Captain. Now, I want the truth from you! Not this trumped-up fairy tale that no one believes for a moment!

SOLDIER: *(In wide-eyed innocence, holding his hands out)* Why —

57

I — I don't understand, sir! I've told you exactly what happened! Certainly you aren't doubting my *word*, sir! *(Drawing himself up)* You must realize I'm a Roman legionnaire! Romans have no reason to lie!

HENRY: Unless it's to their advantage!

SOLDIER: But, sir —

HENRY: *(Vehemently)* Don't give me that "But, Sir" bit. You were about to tell me what actually happened! Then this *(Indicates Lucius)* this — *He* passed a signal on to you with that oh, so convenient coughing spell! *I'll* finish what you were about to say! Suddenly, at dawn, you were startled half out of your wits at the appearance of an angel! He came into view and the earth *shook* with the power of his coming! The brightness of the sun shone from his face; he merely gestured and the stone, that you and your men had so laboriously rolled into the entranceway of the tomb, rolled away! He looked at you, and you all trembled in terrible fear and fell to the earth as dead men, and the Lord Jesus Christ came forth from that tomb! — That's what *really* happened. Isn't it *Captain?* Isn't it?

SOLDIER: *(Shaken, but holding his ground)* No, sir. You have it all — all — wrong, sir. That's not the way it was at all. We were all —

HENRY: *(Impatiently, but resignedly)* I know — you were all asleep! *(Suddenly thinking of something)* Wait! You say you were *all* asleep?

SOLDIER: Yes, sir!

HENRY: And while you were asleep, the disciples came and stole the body?

SOLDIER: Yes, sir! That's exactly how it happened.

HENRY: *(In triumph)* All right, Captain! In the exact words, tell me how you reported to your commanding officer the facts as you have now told me! Tell me how you told him that you, a Roman legionnaire, were asleep on watch! Tell me!

SOLDIER: Why — I — I can't remember the *exact* words. I suppose I merely told him we were all asleep.

HENRY: *(Slowly)* Captain, what is the penalty for falling asleep on watch?

SOLDIER: *(Almost stuttering)* Why, it's — it's death, sir!

HENRY: Death? *(Scathingly)* So, you merely walked up to him and said, "Sir *(Henry salutes)* my men and I were asleep, sir. And while we were sleeping, the disciples came and stole the body from the tomb we were guarding!" Is that what you said, Captain?

SOLDIER: Well, no — not exactly.

HENRY: Shall I tell you exactly what you did? You never went to your commanding officer! You went to the chief priests first and told them the truth of what happened at the tomb that morning! They immediately gave each of you soldiers a large sum of money

58

to spread the story that, as you slept, the disciples came and stole the body of Jesus of Nazareth! Isn't that the truth, Captain? And after you had agreed to this, they promised that should it get back to your superiors that you had been asleep, they, the high priests, would intercede on your behalf and save you from being put to death! Isn't that the way it *really* happened?

SOLDIER: *(With great uncertainty)* Well — I — that is — we —

LUCIUS: *(Coming to his aid)* You can't badger him into saying a thing like that! Anyway, what would it prove?

HENRY: Prove? Why, I want him to admit that he and his men were *not* asleep! I want him to tell the truth about what they saw. They were witnesses to the Resurrection and you know it! He has to admit that it was exactly as I described it! He is the witness that you cannot discredit! I have won, and you know it!

LUCIUS: *(Calmly and confidently)* Not so! You have discredited your own witness!

HENRY: *(Unbelievingly)* I've what?

LUCIUS: You have discredited your own witness!

HENRY: *(Quickly and vehemently)* I have not! What I have said is the truth! How could I have discredited my own witness?

LUCIUS: *(Confidently)* All right, if you insist. Now, you claim that this soldier is a witness to the Resurrection?

HENRY: Yes!

LUCIUS: All right, I accept your description!

HENRY: *(Surprised)* You do? Then I've won!

LUCIUS: *(Calmly)* N-o-t so fast!

HENRY: But you said —

LUCIUS: I *know* what I said! *(Pause)* You claim that he is an eye-witness to the Resurrection?

HENRY: And you said you would accept my description of what happened.

LUCIUS: Exactly! Let's examine that description. Now, you were speaking of this alleged angel that appeared. *You* said, and I agree, he came down, rolled the stone away, sat upon it, and looked at the soldiers. Right?

HENRY: That's right! The tomb was open, and at that moment —

LUCIUS: The soldiers, your words exactly, "fell to the earth as dead men!" How could the soldiers have witnessed this alleged Resurrection or, as you have suggested, be indisputable witnesses, when they — by your testimony — were lying on the ground as dead men? This man's testimony, as well as any other of the watch, is inadmissable in a court of law, as they never saw anyone rise from the dead! *(To the soldier)* Soldier, you are dismissed! Return from whence you came!

(Henry begins to object, but thinks better of it. The soldier turns slowly to leave; Henry calls to him)

HENRY: Captain! *(Soldier pauses)* I just wanted to add — if you had been asleep, how could you have known it was the disciples who, as you claim, "stole" the body? *(Soldier shrugs his shoulders and exits.)*

LUCIUS: *(After soldier has exited)* I want to thank you for making my task much easier.

HENRY: *(Sitting in chair to left, angrily)* He was about to testify to what really happened, when you stopped him!

LUCIUS: *(Feigning innocence)* I? How can you believe such a thing?

HENRY: Believe me, it isn't very difficult!

LUCIUS: Oh, come now. You were beaten on two — no — three counts!

HENRY: What?

LUCIUS: *(Marking them off on his fingers)* First, his admittance, even in the face of execution, that he slept. What court would doubt him? Second, you yourself said he was on the ground as if dead, and, therefore, he couldn't have witnessed a Resurrection! And, third, a competent lawyer could prove that a witness who would accept a bribe and perjure himself is a witness whose testimony would not be reliable, and, therefore, worthless! I told you when you asked for such a witness that you were — *(He shrugs)*

HENRY: I still hold that there is at least one testimony that cannot be discredited. Thomas knows there is one; otherwise why should he have mentioned it? He would have no reason to lead me astray!

LUCIUS: And what makes you think *he* is infallible?

HENRY: Oh, he's not *infallible,* but he *does* know the Bible! That witness is somewhere there, and I'll find him!

LUCIUS: And I say it's a lot of rubbish! We are wasting time! Why not admit you're wrong?

HENRY: *(Straightening)* What? Why, I've only just begun! You realize, don't you, that I haven't called the other women, the disciples, and, don't forget, over —

LUCIUS: *(Martyr-like)* I know — over 500 brethren!

HENRY: *(Gaily)* Well, then, we're wasting time! We'll start with the disciples!

LUCIUS: *(Putting his hands up)* May I suggest something?

HENRY: By all means, do!

LUCIUS: Before you call any of the disciples, hear me out.

HENRY: *(With a gesture)* Be my guest!

LUCIUS: I know you will call Peter first, right?

HENRY: Right!

LUCIUS: Then Thomas?

HENRY: Right!

LUCIUS: *(Earnestly)* You plan to call them all, don't you?

HENRY: Until I find that one witness!

LUCIUS: So, you have finally abandoned your *host* theory for that *lone,* unimpeachable witness?

HENRY: *(Honestly)* Yes, and it could very well be one of the disciples.

LUCIUS: *(Sighing)* Let me save you a great deal of embarrassment and both of us a good deal of time. What lawyer could make the testimony of a ragtag group of Galilean dreamers hold up in court? To begin with *(Lucius counts off his reasons on his fingers),* who could believe them when they say the Son of God allowed a Roman cross to take His life? Everyone saw Him die! Now, the squad of Roman soldiers sent to guard His tomb defy the death penalty to declare that these *same disciples* came and stole the body while they slept! Next, against the sworn word of the chosen leaders of their faith, the Temple priests, who declare that this Jesus of Nazareth was nothing but a confessed blasphemer, these *same disciples,* accused of snatching their dead leader's body and then proclaiming Him as "risen from the dead," are supposed to persuade a court of law that they are telling the truth? Really, Mr. Camden! Why, this one called Peter, the apparent leader of the disciples, even denied with an oath that he never knew his *Great Messiah!* They all ran like sheep when their *Master* was arrested! Now I ask you, do you still believe I would fail to have their testimony discredited? Be sensible!

HENRY: You forget the miracles these same disciples performed in the name of the risen Savior! Doesn't that prove something?

LUCIUS: Doesn't prove a thing to a court of law! Remember how they performed the same miracles *before* their Master went to the cross! You haven't forgotten the seventy that were sent out, have you?

HENRY: *(Bitterly)* Very sure of yourself, aren't you? You take Scripture and twist it, pervert it, misquote it, and —

LUCIUS: Why, Mr. Camden! I call a *spade a spade.* If it gives you cause for doubt, it's only further proof that perhaps I *am* right, after all! You see, I've been around a good deal longer than you, and I can see things that you will never understand! Why, if I were to tell you of —

HENRY: *(At these words, Henry suddenly rises and crosses downstage left)* Wait a minute! *(Suddenly animated)* What was it you just said? You needn't answer. I remember! You've been around a lot longer than I — that's it! Dr. Thomas *was* right!

LUCIUS: *(Confidently)* Well, bully for him!

HENRY: *(Almost as if he were alone, looking out over the audience)* Of course! Why didn't I see it before? It's been there all the time, and I didn't recognize it!

LUCIUS: What under the sun are you mumbling about?

HENRY: *(Now very confidently)* Mumbling? Was I mumbling?

61

(Turns to Lucius) Well, so I was! Forgive me! I wish to call my *last* witness!

LUCIUS: *(Startled, but still confident)* Your *last* witness? Good! Now we can end this silly charade of yours! Who is it this time?

HENRY: *(Crossing slowly to center stage)* You will be quite surprised!

LUCIUS: *(Unruffled)* I can hardly wait! Name your witness! I'll call him!

HENRY: *(In eager anticipation)* Oh, that won't be at all necessary. He is already here! I call Lucius S. Deville to the witness stand!

LUCIUS: *(Completely taken by surprise)* What? Now wait a minute! You can't call me — although I assure you it would do you no good, whatever your purpose! Remember, we agreed that —

HENRY: *(Interrupting eagerly)* I know what we agreed to. No angels and no one of the Trinity! But how does that concern you?

LUCIUS: I claim immunity, for, after all, *I am an angel. (Archly)* Although — ahem — a slightly fallen one, I must admit! Nevertheless, I am —

HENRY: An angel? *(Feigning ignorance)* I've read in the Bible where you are referred to as a serpent, a dragon, a wolf, a raging lion, but — an angel?

LUCIUS: *(Superciliously)* It appears you have neglected your reading of Second Corinthians.

HENRY: Oh?

LUCIUS: Why, your friend Paul himself admitted it! Let me refresh your memory.

HENRY: Please do.

LUCIUS: "For Satan himself is transformed into an angel of light!" So you see. *(Slowly, with emphasis)* I — am — an — *angel! (In triumph)* If *I* am your last witness, which you did *so state*, our little adventure is over — and you lose!

HENRY: *(Reluctantly)* It would seem that way. But haven't you twisted the Scriptures again to suit your purpose? The original tongues are interpreted as saying that you can *transform* yourself into an angel of light.

LUCIUS: Either way it spells failure for you!

HENRY: *(As if defeated, slumps in a chair)* I suppose it makes you feel like a *big* man — defeating an easy mark like me.

LUCIUS: I take little pleasures wherever I find them. Just for the record, what were you going to ask me?

HENRY: It makes no difference now! I'd rather not talk about it!

LUCIUS: Well, it wouldn't have done any good anyhow. So — you finally admit defeat?

HENRY: *(As if in a petulant mood)* Defeat? Not at all! Why should I admit defeat when you have misrepresented yourself to me? You're no more the Devil than I'm King Solomon! *(He begins to talk angrily. Lucius looks startled and completely puzzled.)*

Now, let's drop the masquerade! Just who do you think you're fooling? You don't even look like the Devil! Oh, you've been coached well enough, but the Devil? Don't hand me that!

LUCIUS: *(Completely taken aback)* What? Have you completely lost your mind?

HENRY: No! I've suddenly realized I've been taken in by an imposter! Come on now, confess! Tell me who you really are!

LUCIUS: *(Beginning to be a little impatient)* I tell you I am no imposter! I *am* the Devil!

HENRY: *(Laughing)* The Devil? *(Laughing again)* Haven't you carried this far enough? We've had a good laugh, now let's take off the mask!

LUCIUS: *(Stands)* T — T — Take off my mask? Why you —

HENRY: *(Still laughing)* And I believed you at the beginning when you said *(He imitates Lucius' stentorian tone)* "There is little that goes on in *my* kingdom that I don't know about!" *(Laughing and pointing at Lucius)* Your kingdom! You! — claiming to be a king! *(Laughs even louder)*

LUCIUS: *(Getting very angry)* And I tell you I *am* the ruler of this kingdom and it's mine! Do you hear me? *(Shouting)* THIS IS MY KINGDOM!

HENRY: *(Still laughing and pointing)* Oh, boy! You really took me in, didn't you? First you're a KING — and then you claim you're an angel! Which will you be next — a PRINCE?

LUCIUS: *(Shouting)* Yes, it so happens that I am a Prince! The *Prince of This World!*

HENRY: *(Sarcastically)* Sure! Sure! Why don't you make up your mind? What are you, an angel or a prince? I can't tell in this light! *(Laughs again, almost uncontrollable)*

LUCIUS: *(Shouting)* I tell you I *am* the *prince* of this world!

HENRY: *(Wiping his eyes as he grows weaker, laughing)* What? You've traded in your wings for a scepter?

LUCIUS: *(Frustrated)* What do I have to say to convince you that I am the prince of this world?

HENRY: *(Suddenly quiet)* I believe you're serious!

LUCIUS: *(Still upset)* Serious! Of course, I'm serious!

HENRY: *(Almost apologetically)* Then you *really* are a prince!?

LUCIUS: *(Sitting down triumphantly)* Yes!

HENRY: *(Suddenly triumphant and completely serious, rises, crosses downstage left, turns to Lucius)* Then, since you are a prince, and not an angel, you qualify as a witness, and you won't mind answering my questions?
(Lucius rises angrily, then, checks himself. Remains standing)

LUCIUS: *(Smiling)* Very clever, Henry Camden — very clever! All right, I deserved that! I'm afraid I have underestimated you.

Not that it will do you any good! Ask your questions! I'll play
your little game, but, I warn you — it may prove a bit rough!

HENRY: I'm willing to — as you say — *play* my little game. And —
as for any roughness — two can play *that* little game!

LUCIUS: *(Darkly)* Very brave words! I trust they don't come back to
haunt you! *(Suavely now, as if he had nothing to fear)* By the
way, by what *power* do you intend to force me to witness against
myself?

HENRY: One simple power — *truth!*

LUCIUS: *(Raising his eyebrows)* Truth? *(He pauses, looks at Henry,
then bows mockingly)* The best of luck to you, Henry Camden!

HENRY: You'd best save a bit of luck for yourself, Lucius S. Deville!

LUCIUS: *(Smiling and sitting)* Now who's overconfident?

HENRY: *(Ignoring the sarcasm)* I know that you — and I drop this
"nom de plume" you have come to me with — that you, *Satan,*
are a witness to our Lord's Resurrection and that by your own
words, you shall this night declare it!

LUCIUS: *(Startled)* By my own words? Hah! *(Sitting back)* Tell
me, just how do you intend to do this?

HENRY: *(Calmly)* Patience! It will take but a moment.

LUCIUS: I must say, I certainly admire your confidence — or perhaps
it would best be described as *foolhardiness! (Crosses to chair
stage left and sits.)*

HENRY: Save your clever metaphors for later. *(Henry walks to the
desk and picks up his Bible. He holds it out toward Lucius.)*
I hold in my hand the Bible. Can you — or do you — deny that
this is the Word of God?

LUCIUS: *(Pointing languidly)* Are you planning to use *that* to prove
your point? I can assure you that there is no passage, as you believers call it, in there that proves I was a witness to any resurrection!

HENRY: I am not asking for your exegesis! Answer my question.
Can you deny that this is the Word of God?

LUCIUS: *(With a slight wave of his hand)* If God wants to put His
signature to that literary effort, that's all right with me!

HENRY: I want a straight answer! *Can you deny it?*

LUCIUS: Oh, if it will make you feel more secure — no — I cannot
deny it!

HENRY: *(Relaxing)* Well, I finally got a *straight* answer!

LUCIUS: What can you do with it?

HENRY: *(Sarcastically)* I'm sure you're dying to find out!

LUCIUS: *(Coldly)* Only to teach you a lesson! Get on with it!

HENRY: *(Decisively, with authority)* There are just a few questions
I wish to ask of you and I'll be finished.

LUCIUS: I like your choice of words — "finished"!

HENRY: *(Sitting on the edge of the desk where Lucius had been)*

MEMO

From

Eldon A. Frank

Dear Jean-

How great it was to see you & talk to you, if as briefly as it was, last week! There was so much to say & so little time — I must admit to a large twinge of jealousy toward the people & things that kept us from being able to talk more. I wish I'd had more time to talk to Jon, too — there were really a lot of questions I wanted to ask him & advice I needed, but time just ran out ...

I'm enclosing a copy of the playbook & a Theatre W.Va. playbill from "She

Stoops to Conquer" (which was really very well done – I wish you'd seen it). I will be holding try-outs for "The Visitor" this Sunday – I think. It depends on whether or not a youth musical being presented that night runs very long.

As you can tell, this is not your playbook. I was so impressed with the depth of your insight in your margin notes that I want to be able to refer to them when we rehearse. I want & need your help on this play – so, please, if there's any chance at all, help me! I would like to send you tapes of rehearsals once a week or so & you could listen to them & give me your critical notes in return. As

I said last week, I've got scores
of volunteers & I'm really anxious to
get started. I'm not sure exactly
when we'll present the play, but
I so hope you all can be here to
see it. I'll let you know the date
as soon as I know it.

Hey, dearest friend — I miss
you! May you always walk in His
sunshine ∼ Love,

Eldon

MEMO

From

Eldon A. Frank

Hi —

Please forgive me — I meant to return this long ago. Some items that might be of interest attached.

I spoke at Vienna Baptist last night — a very nice church, Rev. Hadby's a fine man, & I met some wonderful people — also saw many familiar faces, some of whom say "Hi" to you. I'm sure you know who they all are, & some of the names escape me now (I met too many, too fast!).

Had over 30 people volunteer to work on "The Visitor". I'll have tryouts as soon as I get the playbooks. Jean, your comments on the play are excellent! Please expect to be asked for your help — I'll send you your copy back as soon as I get mine.

Love to all,

Eldon

May I remind you of the witnesses who are here. *(Indicates the audience)* I need only to advise you to choose your answers carefully and — if it is not too much to ask — adhere to the truth, if you please!

LUCIUS: There you go again! What's with this word "truth"? Do you think I'm afraid of the truth? I'll prove to you that truth is not a one-sided weapon! You ask me pointedly to stick to the truth. I charge you with the same. We will both adhere strictly to the truth and we shall see which one of us she smiles upon. Agreed?

HENRY: Agreed! *(Slowly folds his arms)* Well, I have really gotten under your skin, haven't I? Let's see — I tricked you into the witness chair. You have acknowledged that the Bible is the Word of God. Now, you have challenged me to a contest of truth! It seems to me you've lost the fuses to your most potent weapons! Could it be you have let down your guard just a bit?

LUCIUS: You know, the trouble with you believers is that just when you think my teeth have been pulled, you find yourself all chewed up! Don't forget, my confident young adversary, I know every word in that book you wave so bravely — and I know how to use it!

HENRY: I don't doubt it a bit! Shall we test the power of that Word?

LUCIUS: *(Nodding)* Be my guest!

HENRY: Let's visit the Garden of Eden first.

LUCIUS: *(Tauntingly)* Ah, yes — the scene of my greatest triumph!

HENRY: *(As if he didn't hear)* Is it true that you entered the Garden of Eden?

LUCIUS: As a matter of fact — and please note that I am adhering to the truth — yes, I did!

HENRY: And how did you manage that? The Garden was perfect in every way and, therefore, you were not allowed there!

LUCIUS: Now you know that as well as I!

HENRY: I want to hear it in your own words, so there will be no mistake in the matter of motive, etc. You can understand, I'm sure.

LUCIUS: Oh, I don't mind telling the truth. I am quite proud of my subtlety! *(Pause)* It's true, I was not allowed in the Garden, so I had to, shall we say, "borrow" a ticket! The woman Eve, like all women, was fascinated by beauty, so I chose the serpent's body to gain entrance to the Garden and to get near to her. Of course, you know it was a good choice, as the serpent was probably the most subtle and knowledgeable creature in the Garden — next to man. He was tremendously attractive and knew how to talk to a woman as well!

HENRY: Very clever.

LUCIUS: *(Suavely)* Thank you! Well — gaining entrance was the most difficult part of my plan. Eve was simply a "pushover!"

HENRY: How interesting! Then, of course, you lied to her!

LUCIUS: *(Sitting up belligerently)* Lied? I wouldn't say that! Consider the evidence. I merely asked whether God had give her permission to eat of every fruit of the garden! Naturally she said He had, but that there was one exception — the fruit of the tree in the center of the garden. She then said that God had told her the penalty for eating that fruit would be death.

HENRY: And you *then* lied to her.

LUCIUS: You keep saying I lied! Why? I merely told her that she wouldn't die! The truth of my statement is borne out in the fact that she did eat of the fruit and she certainly didn't drop dead! Now did she?

HENRY: But what God meant was —

LUCIUS: *(Quickly interrupting)* AAH! AAH! AAH! It doesn't say "well, I meant such and such!" It says simply — "you will surely die!" Right? Now, you've asked me to tell the story in my own words — let me! *(Henry waits)* Then I told her the facts. The reason God didn't want them to eat of that fruit was because if they did, they would become like gods, knowing good and evil. Now, I ask you — wasn't everything I said the truth?

HENRY: You don't really want me to answer that, do you?

LUCIUS: Well — anyway, the record is there! I didn't force her to take the fruit and eat it! She did it all by herself, the silly woman! I merely laid the facts before her! Don't you see the beauty of my plan? You must admit it worked beautifully!

HENRY: *(Sarcastically)* Yeah — a real classic!

LUCIUS: *(With mock sorrow)* Aw — I see you don't share my view.

HENRY: *There* you are speaking the *truth!* You knew very well that to disobey God's command meant death! You also knew that all of humanity stood to be marked for death!

LUCIUS: *(Earnestly)* Now you get the picture! Can't you see the beauty of it all? Just as you said — a real *classic!*

HENRY: You twist the truth of the Scriptures and now you're twisting *my* words! But you've told me what I wanted to hear. I wanted to hear it from your own lips. Now that I have, you won't mind my preparing my next question, will you?

LUCIUS: Not at all! But how do you expect to prove your point by parading my victories?

HENRY: *Are* they victories?

LUCIUS: You *are* a difficult one to convince, aren't you? Rave on!

HENRY: Because of man's fallen state, he needed to be redeemed. In the fullness of time, I am sure you know exactly what I mean, God sent His Son to redeem His people. Now, you knew that Jesus came to die for all humanity, did you not?

LUCIUS: Are you asking questions or putting words in my mouth?

66

HENRY: Come, now — you're evading the question! Answer me! You knew that Jesus came to die for all humanity?

LUCIUS: What has this to do with my being a witness to a resurrection?

HENRY: *(Rising and crossing in front of desk to stage right)* You are still avoiding the question. Must I quote Scripture to prove you know? You can save a great deal of time by giving me your answer with a simple word.

LUCIUS: *(Resigned)* Oh, all right. We all know that God's Son came to die for all humanity! Yes, I know that is true! But it still doesn't prove my witness to His alleged resurrection!

HENRY: I haven't claimed it does! My next question may throw a little light on my reason for ascertaining your knowledge of His death. Why did you try to stop Christ from giving His life?

LUCIUS: *(Sits up straight)* What? *Me* try to stop Him? What do you mean?

HENRY: You surely aren't forgetting your visit in the wilderness, are you?

LUCIUS: Oh — that.

HENRY: *(Satisfied)* Yes, that! First you tempted Christ with hunger, but that trick failed.

LUCIUS: I couldn't see any reason for Him to be hungry! After all, He only had to change a stone into bread! It would have been quite simple. He *was* the Son of God and could easily have done so!

HENRY: You're very clever with words! But the next two temptations are not so easily dealt with! They both are concerned with the same thing, so I ask them together! Why did you ask the Lord to prove He was immune to death by leaping from the pinnacle of the Temple? And why did you offer Him the kingdoms of the world if He would bow down and worship you?

LUCIUS: *(Not so sure of himself)* Why — that's easy! *(Pause)* Yes! I can answer your question. I simply wanted to spare Him the agony of the cross! Prove Himself the Son of God before all those people standing in front of the Temple by surviving such a leap, miraculously, and everyone would follow Him!

HENRY: *(Sarcastically)* You really had His good at heart, didn't you?

LUCIUS: And the offer of the kingdoms of the world, which were *mine* to give, also would spare Him the necessity of the cross. He could have the whole world simply by bowing down and worshiping me! Why go to the cross when He could claim the world He sought by simply acknowledging me! Now what could be simpler than that?

HENRY: I see what you mean. *(Henry pretends to see Lucius' plan in a new light)* Your way *would* win Christ the whole world without the necessity of rejection, crucifixion, resurrection, and depending on the preaching of the Word.

LUCIUS: That's it! What could have been simpler?

HENRY: *(Feigning wonder)* When you put it that way, it doesn't seem possible that anyone could choose otherwise! You might be evil, but that really was clever of you!

LUCIUS: *(Flattered)* I'm glad you can see it my way. I've misjudged you!

HENRY: *(Still in feigned wonder)* But He turned you down cold!

LUCIUS: *(Satisfied)* It is a matter of record!

HENRY: *(Still pretending)* He chose the hard way! Rejection and enmity of His people.

LUCIUS: Right!

HENRY: *(Slowly and thoughtfully)* He chose the flogging with all the pain. And the crucifixion with its shame and agony. And the resurrection which so few ever believed. And the foolishness of preaching!! *(He turns to Lucius and says with great feeling)* Are you sure He *did* choose all this instead of your offer?

LUCIUS: *(Slowly and in the same voice — without suspecting Henry's trap)* Of *course* I'm sure. I was *there!* I saw all my plans go for nothing! Everything I had worked for! Probably my most costly defeat!

HENRY: *(Suddenly smiling)* And you can add another defeat to your list!

LUCIUS: *(As if awakening)* What?

HENRY: You just lost our *little* contest! You just testified to the resurrection of Jesus Christ!

LUCIUS: *(Standing suddenly)* I did what? You're dreaming!

HENRY: *(Happily)* Oh, are we back to dreams again? No, it's not a dream! You just admitted, before *(Indicates audience)* witnesses, that Christ arose from the dead!

LUCIUS: *(Thinking desperately)* I couldn't have! It's some sort of trick! You tricked me! *(Pacing about)* You put words in my mouth! It won't hold up in a court of law!

HENRY: *(Standing and speaking firmly)* Oh, come now! You not only claimed that Christ arose, but the very evidence you so willingly gave convicts you! You offered Christ a bribe, hoping to prevent His crucifixion and the resurrection that followed! You knew that if He did go to the cross, it would spell the end of you! You can't deny it, Lucius S. Deville!! Deny it if you dare! *(He stands defiantly before Lucius)*

LUCIUS: *(Fairly gnashing his teeth)* I do! I — *(He stops in mid-sentence. His upraised hand slowly drops to his side and gradually a smile begins to replace his look of frustration and hatred. In a few short moments he is again the smooth, suave Lucius.)* So, you think you have won a *great victory?* This was just a skirmish! I

68

have my eye on you, and I will see to it that you get my special, personal attention! *(He begins to back toward the door)* Perhaps the next time you won't be so fortunate! You have not heard the last of Lucius S. Deville, Henry Camden! Everywhere you go, everything you do, everything you want, I will be there, watching — waiting — in the shadows. *(He exits slowly.)*

(Henry suddenly sits down at his desk, breathing out a huge sigh and wiping his forehead with his sleeve. Suddenly he begins to laugh. He laughs loudly and long. Slowly he calms down and, still chuckling, he stretches, yawns, and finally lays his head on his arm. With a final chuckle, he falls asleep. Suddenly the telephone rings. He slowly wakens and answers it.)

HENRY: *(Sleepily)* Hello? *(Pause. He sits up quickly)* Oh, Professor Thomas! *(Pause)* No, I was just sitting at my desk, working a few minutes. *(Pause)* Wait, I'll look. *(He sets the phone down and walks over to the door. He picks up an umbrella and carries it back to the desk. He picks up the phone.)* Yes, you left it here, sir. *(Pause)* Yes, sir! *(Pause)* Good night, sir. *(He begins to put the phone down and suddenly shouts into the mouthpiece)* Oh — Professor! I nearly forgot! I know who the witness is. *(Pause)* Yes! *(Pause)* No, I'll tell you in class tomorrow. *(Pause)* No, I'm sure! *(Pause)* Yes, Good night, sir!

(He sets the phone back in its cradle. He stands, stretches, begins to walk over to the bed, and stops suddenly and looks at the door. He slowly walks over to it, seeing it is open. He closes it, after first looking out into the hall. He starts to go back toward the bed, stops, looks around at the closed door, looks over at the desk, shakes his head, and turns back to the bed.)

(Curtain)

CHRISTMAS WORE WOOL MITTENS

Characters
    Fred Mason — vice-president of an airline and father of six children
    Dorothy Mason — wife and mother
    Mabel — daughter, eleven
    June — daughter, thirteen
    Mary — daughter, fifteen
    Jack — son, seventeen
    Henry — son, nineteen
    Larry — son, twenty-five
    Nancy — Larry's wife, twenty-two

Time
    Christmas Eve, the present

Place
    Living room of the Mason home *(see Fig. 1)*.

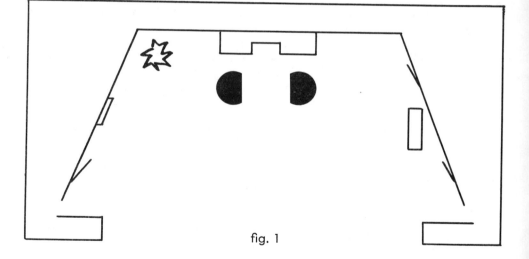

fig. 1

(As the scene opens, Mr. and Mrs. Mason are seated by the fireplace. He is reading the paper, and she is knitting a pair of mittens. Mabel is trimming a small tree, while Henry stares out the window.
    June, Mary, and Jack are upstairs getting ready to leave for the airport to pick up Larry, who has been away from home for four years.

This is to be his first Christmas at home since he graduated from the School of Mining and accepted a job in Alaska.

Excitement is at fever pitch as all wait anxiously for word from the airport that Larry has arrived.)

HEN: Boy, dad! It looks like it might snow. Will that hold up Larry's flight?

FATH: Henry! That's about the tenth time you've asked that. If the snow holds up Larry's plane, we'll hear from the airport. Now come away from that window! You're *making me nervous!* Why don't you busy yourself with something? Help Mabel finish the tree. Anything — but get away from that window! *(Henry helps Mabel.)*

MOTH: Now, Fred, the boy is just anxious. And so are you. So don't shout at him.

FATH: *(Pause)* I guess you're right, Dorothy. I am on edge. I'm sorry, son. Guess we're all a bit excited.

HEN: Aw — that's all right, dad.

(Everyone is quiet. Father looks up from paper and watches mother knitting.)

FATH: Aren't those the same mittens you were working on last Christmas?

MOTH: Fred, don't be silly — of course not! I sent that pair to Larry last year.

FATH: Dorothy, I can't understand you. What makes you think Larry wears woolen mittens up there? He needs something warmer.

MOTH: Larry has always liked the mittens I made for him. I'm sure they were useful.

FATH: Mark my word — I'll bet they were put away and never used all year. Why, up there they use leather gloves with sheepskin lining. Not that your mittens aren't good, dear, but they're not practical for Alaska.

MOTH: We'll see.

(Jack, June, and Mary dash in.)

JUNE: We're ready to go, dad.

MARY: Shall we leave now?

JACK: I'll get the car out.

FATH: Now, wait a minute! Larry said he'd call from the airport. So all of you just sit down. Amuse yourselves with something. Better yet, help your mother by setting the table.

MOTH: Oh, Fred, I can do that while they go for Larry.

JUNE: No, Mother, we'll do it. *(The three exit to dining room.)*

MOTH: *(Pause)* Fred, I'm worried. Wasn't Larry due in on Flight 16 at 5:30? It's almost six now.

FATH: Yes, but holiday traffic is always a bit late — and especially with the uncertain weather.

MOTH: Well, I'd feel reassured if you'd just call the airport and find out when they expect to land.

FATH: Now, Dorothy *(Pause)*, all right *(Dials number)*. Hello — Ralph? This is Fred. Any word on Flight 16? *(Pause)* Uh, uh. *(Pause)* Uh, uh. *(Pause)* Well, let me know as soon as something shows up. Bye. *(Puts phone down with worried look.)* Mabel — Henry — see if you can help the others in the kitchen.

MOTH: *(As they leave, she puts down knitting.)* What is it, Fred?

FATH: Nothing to get excited about, Dorothy. I just didn't want to alarm the children. *(Pause)* Flight 16 has lost contact with the tower over Pittsburgh. She gave her last position as being east and south of Pittsburgh and said she was icing up.

MOTH: Do you think there's a chance they'll have to land out in Pennsylvania?

FATH: Yes — but having lost radio contact, our only hope is that they are receiving and are able to follow the radio beam. *(Pause)* Come now, Dorothy, lots of planes lose contact temporarily. Everything will be all right.

(Children burst in from dining room.)

ALL: Can we get out the Christmas candles? We can eat by candlelight. May we sprinkle artificial snow on the tablecloth? How about hanging the Christmas bell over the table? And maybe we can string some popcorn. . . .

MOTH: Yes-yes-yes-yes-yes! Now, back to work with you. *(Exit noisily)* *(Pause)* Fred, I'm terribly worried.

FATH: *(Walks over and touches her shoulder)* Nonsense, dear. In a moment that phone will ring and it will be Larry, yelling for a ride home. *(Phone rings)* See — what did I tell you? That's probably him now. *(Picks up receiver)* Yes, Ralph. *(Pause)* Where? *(Pause)* Any survivors? *(Pause)* Thank you, Ralph — no — good night. *(Replaces receiver, his face blank with shock)*

MOTH: Fred — Flight 16?

FATH: Yes. *(Long pause)* It crashed just east of Pittsburgh!

MOTH: No survivors?

FATH: *(Shakes head)* None.

MOTH: Oh, Fred! *(Buries her face)* Our boy! *(He comes over and grasps her hand)* How are we going to tell the children?

FATH: I don't know. But we'll have to do it now before they hear it on the news or something. *(Long pause)*

MOTH: Call them, dear.

FATH: *(Crosses to door)* Kids, come in here. *(They rush in with shouts of "He's here"; "Was it Larry?" etc. Upon seeing their mother weeping, all fall silent.)*

FATH: I want you to listen quietly. We've just received word from the airport that Larry's plane *(Knock on door)*

LAR: Hey, open up in there!

72

ALL: Larry! (*All rush to door. Larry comes in followed by Nancy. All gather around, not seeming to notice her. Finally they quiet down.*)

MOTH: But, Larry — how — when — did —

LAR: What's the matter, mom? You look as if you were seeing a ghost.

MOTH: (*Clinging to him*) Oh, Larry — Larry — we thought you were dead.

LAR AND CHILDREN: *Dead?*

FATH: Son, Flight 16 crashed outside of Pittsburgh.

LAR: But we weren't on Flight 16.

FATH: Then how *did* you get here?

LAR: I sent you a telegram. We missed Flight 16 but picked up an emergency ride on one of the company's freight runs. Not exactly first class, but acceptable.

FATH: We?

LAR: Nancy and I.

MOTH: Nancy?

LAR: Nancy!!! (*As if suddenly remembering her*)

NAN: (*Coming forward*) That's me — Nancy (*Comic salute*) reporting for duty, Captain.

LAR: (*Puts his arm around her*) Forgive me, sweetheart.

ALL: Sweetheart —

LAR: Well, isn't it all right to call my wife sweetheart?

ALL: Wife?

LAR: This isn't exactly the way I'd planned to tell you, but Nancy and I were married a week ago today. Mother, I brought you a special Christmas present — Instant Daughter!

MOTH: (*Embraces Nancy*) I warn you — he's just an overgrown boy — just like his father.

NAN: I've looked forward to this moment — mother. Now I'm beginning to understand why Larry is the fine man he is. (*Reaches out to father*) And hi to you, dad.

FATH: Welcome, Nancy. I see Larry inherited one thing from me anyway — now we have two Mrs. Americas in the family!

LAR: Nancy, this is Mabel — June — Mary — Jack — and Henry. (*They embrace or shake hands and exchange greetings as introduced.*)

FATH: Larry, you mentioned a telegram. We never received it.

LAR: You didn't? (*Turns to Nancy with mock seriousness, but she has already started looking through her purse.*)

NAN: I knew I forgot something. (*Hands paper to him*) In the excitement it got buried. (*Suddenly, with hand to mouth*) Larry! Did I turn off the gas?

MOTH: Now you sound like me.

NAN: Well, it was a bit hectic after we missed the plane. I just forgot in all the confusion.

MOTH: Which reminds me — how *did* you miss the plane?

LAR: It was all on account of those mittens you knitted for me last year, mom.

MOTH: What? Now really — Larry.

NAN: No, mother. Not really. Tell her what happened, Larry.

LAR: Well, it's a bit complicated, but it does involve those mittens you sent me.

MOTH: The ones your father insists are utterly useless in Alaska.

LAR: Useless! Far from it, dad. They fit beautifully inside my sheepskin gloves. I wouldn't go on the job without them.

NAN: You see, some of Larry's work must be done where heavy gloves are too awkward. So Larry just slips off the leather ones and his hands are still protected by the knitted mittens — that's why they're so handy. They're flexible and still keep his hands warm.

LAR: The other men are doing the same now. So you see, when I wore a hole in one of the mittens, I thought I'd bring it along for mother to mend with her matching yarn.

NAN: And wouldn't you know it — halfway to the airport, Larry discovered he'd forgotten the mittens.

LAR: I just had to go back and get them.

NAN: I tried to talk him out of doing it — we could have mailed them later. But — back he went.

LAR: So, because we did, we missed Flight 16 and — *(Silence)*

FATH: *(Handing mother her knitting)* Keep right on knitting, mother!
(Curtain)

FAITH OR FOLLY

Characters

Mr. Marsten — father
Mrs. Marsten — mother
Janice — daughter, eighteen
Arthur — son, sixteen
Angela — Janice's college roommate
Miss Baker — Janice's teacher

Time and Place

Scene I — Late summer. Dining room in Marsten home.
Scene II — Weeks later. Living room in Marsten home.
Scene III — Same time. Room in college dormitory.
Scene IV — Weeks later. Living room in Marsten home.
Scene V — Christmas Day. Dining room in Marsten home.

This one-act play, in five scenes is designed to be performed in three simple settings.

Scenes I and V consist of a dining room table with four chairs, with the downstage side of the table empty so that the characters are either facing the audience or in profile (*see Fig.* 1). Scenes II and IV can be equally simple. At stage left place a living room table, two easy chairs, and a floor lamp. Stage right use a small table with a telephone on it and a chair beside it (*see Fig.* 2). Scene III may be set up with a small table, two chairs, and two single cots (*see Fig.* 3).

If there is no curtain available, the scene changes may be made quietly during the Narrator's reading. Narrator may stand directly in front of scene or to the side. If a curtain is used, highlight Narrator with a spotlight.

Keep properties at a minimum so that no elaborate preparation is necessary. It is the dialogue that makes the play effective, not the scenery.

NAR: This is the story of the Marsten family. Who are the Marstens? Well, they are a family who do not really exist — or they could be the family down the street. What makes them of particular interest to us is that soon each member of the household will come face to face with a "turning point" in his or her life. To set the scene, let's have a brief summary of the events leading up to the present moment as the Marsten family steps before you. (*As each member is called, he/she comes in and takes his/her place for Scene I.*)

75

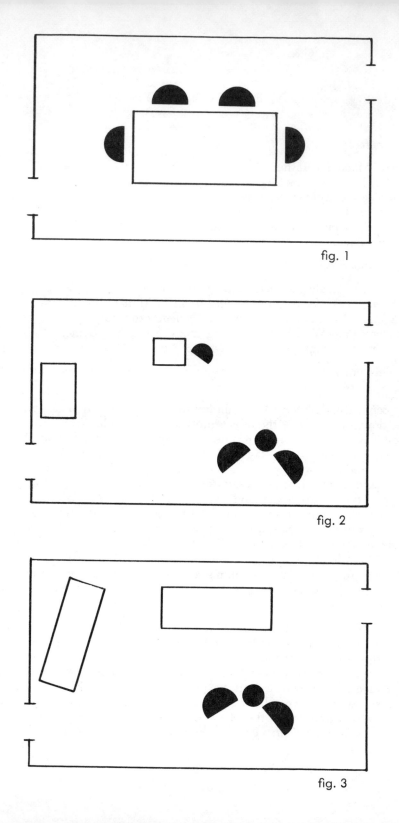

fig. 1

fig. 2

fig. 3

Mr. Marsten is an executive of an electronics firm. His whole life has been dedicated to his work, and as a result, he is a good provider of all the material things that life offers. His philosophy of life, however, stems from an atheistic view of eternity, and the natural fruits of this are evident in many ways, the most apparent being his attempt to drown his problems in alcohol.

Mrs. Marsten was once a teen-ager who vibrantly defended her faith, but in the years following her marriage to one militantly opposed to Christianity, she has allowed herself to be drawn away to the point where she no longer claims any allegiance to Christian ideals. Her faith has been replaced by a selfish indifference to the normal callings of a good life; gradually she has become a bickering shrew whose venom is primarily aimed at her husband's main weakness — drinking.

Janice, like her brother Arthur, is a victim of this parental discord, as evidenced by her unrest and insecurity. She is about to leave for college where she hopes to find escape from parents whom she no longer respects.

Arthur has found his escape from the explosive atmosphere of his home by burying himself in the world of science and research. Arthur believes that science alone holds the answers to all of life's problems. He has inherited not only his father's intelligence, but also shares his spiritual vacuum, finding his outlet in agnosticism. To complicate his life even more, Arthur is contemplating leaving home, although he is only sixteen.

Scene I

Our story begins on a day in late summer. The Marstens are eating the evening meal; it is a bit special, as Janice leaves for college in the morning.

JAN: This is great, mother — you cooked such a wonderful meal for my last dinner at home.

FATH: *(Reaching across table for bread)* That's something she never does for me.

MOTH: *(Snapping)* Perhaps I would if you'd leave and promise never to come back.

FATH: *(Viciously)* And where would you be if I did? You'd starve.

MOTH: I'd get plenty from you and you know it. At least I wouldn't have to put up with your drunken brawling.

FATH: *(With rising temper)* Without you around, there would be no need to drink. And as for getting plenty from me — before I'd let you get one red cent, I'd rot in jail.

JAN: *(Yelling)* Stop it! Stop it! Stop it! My last day at home, and you have to spend it yelling at one another. *(Pause)* Mother — please. Dad — can't you understand how important it is that our last evening together be a nice one?

77

FATH: *(Mumbling through mouthful of food)* You don't have to teach me how to act in my own home.

MOTH: *(Shaking fork at him)* You could learn plenty. That is, if your alcohol-fogged brain could absorb it.

FATH: Why don't you get off my back? One drink with the boys and you call me a rum-sot.

MOTH: One drink! Don't make me laugh!

JAN: *(Trying to change the subject)* You know who I'm rooming with this year at college? You remember Angela Peters — the girl who won the bowling cup last year? Well, she's going to teach me how to bowl!

MOTH: *(As if Janet hadn't even spoken)* And just for the record, I cooked a pretty good meal for you last Father's Day, didn't I?

ART: *(Putting his fork down)* How could he forget it? You lectured him through the whole meal on how big a failure he was as a father!

MOTH: I was merely pointing out that —

JAN: Do we have to bring up all the unpleasant things from the past?

FATH: Janice — your mother could lecture a saint and never —

MOTH: *(Scoffing)* Now he's comparing himself to the saints! Ha! You think I don't know about you and all your office parties with all the drinking and those pretty secretaries? People have talked, you know.

FATH: Here we go again! To hear you talk, one would think we were running a tavern filled with pretty barmaids. It so happens that I'm a $35,000 a year executive with great responsibilities. Do you think they pay me that just to organize wild parties?

MOTH: Are you trying to deny that you've had some p-r-e-t-t-y slick parties down there at your office? I've heard you bragging to your friends. And you're very careful never to invite me.

FATH: Sure we've had some real nice office parties — but there's never been a lot of drinking. As for inviting you — you've always refused.

ART: He has you there, mother. I've heard him ask you plenty of times.

MOTH: You keep out of this!

FATH: That's right, son; it doesn't do any good to prove your mother wrong. As for pretty secretaries — Mrs. Rogers, my secretary, is a widow with three boys in college. She's efficient and well worth the salary we pay her. And she's far from "pretty."

JAN: We've been over this a thousand times before. Why can't we have a quiet, peaceful dinner?

FATH: Tell it to your mother. She's the one who has the wild imagination.

JAN: Daddy, you started it with your remark about not having a dinner like this in your honor.

FATH: So now it's me! Janice — you're old enough to know what I've been putting up with all these years. No matter what I say, it will lead to an argument with your mother.

MOTH: If you'd come through that door just once without liquor on your breath, perhaps I —

JAN: Mother — may I be excused from the table?

MOTH: I was about to serve dessert.

JAN: I don't care for any dessert, thank you.

MOTH: I made it especially for you, Janice.

JAN: Did you plan all these arguments for me too?

FATH: Don't get smart with us, young lady!

JAN: All I want is to be excused.

FATH: *(Banging the table)* Then, by thunder, get going! *(Janice rises)*

MOTH: So this is the thanks I get for all my work! I cook and —

JAN: *(Quickly)* Mother, thank you for the delicious dinner. I think I'll finish my packing. *(She exits)*

FATH: Now, I hope you're satisfied. Her last day at home and you had to make your daily scene. *(He storms out)*

(Curtain)

Scene II

NAR: A number of weeks have passed. Janice is away at college. It is evening in the Marsten home, and Mr. Marsten is reading the evening paper. Mrs. Marsten is sewing and half listening to Arthur as he completes a telephone conversation with a classmate. In a moment the first event will occur that will cause this family to pause as God begins to make His presence felt.

ART: *(On the telephone)* That's what I told Chuck. *(Pause)* No, I think this is the best way, and we won't hurt anyone's feelings. *(Pause)* Okay, I'll see you at Lab tomorrow. So long, Ted. *(He hangs up receiver and thinks for a moment.)*

MOTH: What was that all about?

ART: Oh — our Science Club has to get rid of one of our members who just isn't working out.

MOTH: Why? What's wrong?

ART: Well — it's happened quite a number of times. Our Science Club is doing some research on Darwin's Origin of the Species, and we made a report on it in Biology class today. We've only met once on the subject, but Mr. Callan wanted us to make a short report on what we'd discussed at our first meeting.

MOTH: What's that got to do with getting rid of one of your members?

ART: That's what I'm coming to. Right in the middle of our report, Michael Brandt, the president of the Hi-Y group that meets every week, got up and interrupted Chuck, who was making the report. He challenged Chuck on a statement about how Darwin claimed

79

that evolution was the only answer to man's present existence. Can you imagine this character claiming that Darwin was wrong and that *God* created the whole universe. He claimed that man didn't evolve but was created by God just as he looks today.

FATH: *(Has put down his paper)* We have a couple like that down at work. First they say that their God is love and that He created everything. Then when we ask if He made wars and earthquakes and disease, they try to sell us on the idea that there's a big boogeyman called the devil who causes all those bad things. Well, if this God they talk about made everything, then He must have made this devil too. Then they go off into a big deal about sin and salvation. You ask them for proof and they tell you it's "inside." Well, I've got something inside me that tells me they're a bunch of nuts.

MOTH: *(Calmly)* They are as entitled to their beliefs as you are to yours.

FATH: *(In powerful tones)* Oh — the great oracle speaks. *(Scoffing)* That's right, you used to have some silly ideas along those lines when I first met you. Your father and mother were real pious, weren't they? They sure tried to break us up, I remember. It wasn't too long after I took you away from them that you gave up this idiotic idea of "Our Heavenly *Father!*"

MOTH: I realize that I was weak and very much in love in those days. I left a lot of wonderful things behind when I married you.

FATH: Left a lot of wonderful things? Listen, woman — look around you! You were living in a crummy three-room apartment. Now you have a $50,000 home of your own. Your parents drove a five-year-old Ford and you're driving your own Imperial. You were eating hamburger and drinking milk. Now you eat steak and drink good, red wine. Don't talk to me about the wonderful things you left behind. And what did you pay for that dress you're wearing?

MOTH: I'm remembering the more *simple* things. A dish of ice cream was a once-a-week luxury. A pair of new shoes from Sears and Roebuck was an event that held its glow for weeks. My father's quiet prayers when things were not going right, and his wonderful prayers of thanks when God helped him through a difficult decision —

FATH: Oh, fine. Now you're going back to that mess again.

MOTH: I'm only thinking that Michael Brandt is brave enough and strong enough to stand up for what he believes. Now he'll be made to drop out of a club to which he was probably proud to belong.

FATH: Well, there's no room in this modern world for that ancient superstition of *God!* Christianity will never bring Michael Brandt success, that's for sure.

80

MOTH: I'm not proud of what I am now. Sure, I have a beautiful home, beautiful clothes, good food, and a big car. But I also have bickering, unhappiness, disrespectful children, a cursing, drinking husband. I've lost the only thing in life that ever brought me a feeling of peace — simple faith in a loving God.

FATH: You make me sick! You're a good candidate for that hymn-singing bunch of hypocrites down the street in that — that — church, whatever its name is.

MOTH: Maybe I am a good candidate. Perhaps this Sunday I will go and find out.

ART: *(Mockingly, to his father)* Oh, no — now see what you've done. She's going holy!

(They both burst into laughter)

(Curtain)

Scene III

NAR: So, a small incident has stirred memories of the past in the heart and mind of Mrs. Marsten. Is it possible that this slender contact with the past will be quickly broken by the ridicule that comes from her jeering son and husband? But, so as not to anticipate, we will leap the miles and visit Janice as she struggles with her studies, new disciplines, and, what is most important, her reaction to that moment when God brings into her life a "turning point." We find her, early in the evening, in her dormitory room. Angela, her roommate, is helping her with an assignment which is due the next day.

ANG: Try it again from "To this we might add."

JAN: To this we might add the ingredient of a happy and wholesome home life. There is nothing that so promotes — so promotes — so promo — *(Throwing herself in a chair)* Oh, what's the use? What do I know about a happy and wholesome home life?

ANG: *(Coming over to her)* Sorry, Jan — I wish I could help you.

JAN: *(Looking up at her)* You're sweet, Angela. Maybe I'll try again in the morning.

ANG: You know I'll do anything to help you with your report.

JAN: I know — and I appreciate it. *(Looking at her watch)* Golly, I have to be at Miss Baker's in ten minutes.

ANG: And I have to attend that bowling team meeting. *(Dashing for the door)* I'll see you later. Bye. *(She dashes out the door, nearly trampling Miss Baker who was about to knock)* Oh, hello, Miss Baker!

MISS B: Hello, Angela. Where to in such a hurry?

ANG: *(Breathlessly)* I'm sorry to have nearly knocked you down, Miss Baker. I'm on my way to a bowling team meeting.

MISS B: *(Laughing)* I'm just thankful you weren't carrying a bowling ball. Well, don't let me keep you. Good night.

81

ANG: Good night.

MISS B: *(Turning to Janice)* I just left a prayer meeting, and I realized that I'd pass by your dormitory. I thought I'd save you the trip over to my office, that is, if you don't mind our talking here in your room.

JAN: Not at all, Miss Baker. Do come in and sit down. *(Miss Baker sits down. Janice shuts the door and follows.) (Pause)* I feel somewhat awkward, remembering the last talk we had. I'm afraid I unloaded all my griefs and problems on you.

MISS B: You shouldn't feel that way, Janice. I am honored that you wanted to share them with me.

JAN: *(Startled)* Honored? But all I told you were terrible things about my family, and especially my father.

MISS B: I'm glad you did. It answers many questions that have been puzzling me. You see, Janice, I know what you are capable of doing in your studies. Everything points to an "A" student. It puzzled me why you weren't working up to your capabilities.

JAN: *(Puzzled, slightly)* Are you saying that what happens to me at home affects my studies?

MISS B: Yes, Janice. You see, what parents are to their children has a great deal to do with what those children become. In your case, your mother, and a great deal of what your father is, have had a strong influence on how you are reacting to the disciplines here at college.

JAN: If this is true, you must have a wonderful father, Miss Baker.

MISS B: Oh, yes, Janice. My Father is kind and understanding, and He loves me very much. As long as I have known Him, He's seen to it that I have never wanted for anything.

JAN: *(Passionately)* Oh, Miss Baker, that must be just — just — just heavenly! I'm so happy for you. No wonder you're so — well, such a nice person. You've had a father who loves you — *(Suddenly)* Wait a minute! You said your father is kind and that he *LOVES* you! How can that be? I was reading the write-up about you in last year's yearbook and it said that you were an orphan.

MISS B: That's right, Janice.

JAN: Well — how — where?

MISS B: I was speaking of my Heavenly Father.

JAN: *(Doubtfully)* Heavenly Father? You mean — God?

MISS B: Yes, Janice. He's my Father and He can be yours too.

JAN: *(Still puzzled)* He can? I don't know what you mean, Miss Baker. The only time I ever heard God mentioned around our home was when my dad was drunk or angry. Of course when I was little, mother used to send my brother and me to Sunday school, but I remember only a little of that.

MISS B: I understand, Janice. But God is so much more than just a word.

82

JAN: *(Leaning toward her)* Miss Baker, I don't know how to say this. but — if I knew God, does that mean that some day I'd be like — like you?

MISS B: *(Smiling)* I'm afraid that I'm not the best of patterns, Janice. But if you mean will God fill your life with meaning and purpose — yes!

JAN: Then I *want* to know Him. Will you tell me what I have to do?

MISS B: *(Opening her Bible)* Yes, Janice, I will. *(Janice comes over and sits on the floor beside Miss Bakes as the scene ends.)*

(Curtain)

Scene IV

NAR: What a change! The letters that Janice writes to her mother are now filled with her new-found faith. And what has this turn of events meant to Mrs. Marsten? How has Mr. Marsten reacted to the news? The truth is, Mrs. Marsten has wrestled with the problem of how to tell him for a number of weeks. She has read and reread Janice's letters, and a numbing fear clutches at her heart as she searches for a way to reveal to her husband the new and vibrant purpose that now fills the life of their daughter. Finally she makes her decision! This very evening she will reveal the contents of the letters to Mr. Marsten. We find her in the living room, waiting for him. She has all Janice's letters on the table beside her. At the moment her tear-filled eyes are reading the first letter in which Janice revealed her encounter with Jesus Christ.

(Mrs. Marsten, seated stage right, is reading letter. Suddenly she crushes it to her lips. At that moment Mr. Marsten walks in. He slams down his briefcase and looks at her. She has risen to her feet but still holds letter in her hands.)

FATH: Well — aren't you going to smell my breath? Sure, I stopped off with the boys. Well? Why don't you yell at me? What's the matter with you? You sick?

MOTH: Yes — I guess I am sick. I've been sick for a long time.

FATH: What's this? The martyr act? Well, it won't work. I've known you long enough —

MOTH: *(Interrupting)* Jim!

FATH: Jim? You haven't called me that in years. *(Noticing letter)* What's that in your hand?

ART: *(Enters)* I'm home. See you at dinner. *(He begins to walk by his mother and notices her strangeness. He looks at his dad.)* What's wrong with her highness?

FATH: I guess it's something in that letter. *(He snatches it from her. She stands silent and motionless.)*

ART: What is it, dad?

FATH: *(Preoccupied)* Shut up and let me read. *(As he reads, he be-*

83

comes visibly agitated and angry. Finally he tears the letter to bits.) So that's it. We're putting out good money to send her to college to get an education, and all she does is learn about this Jesus you used to moon about when we were first married. Well, I won't stand for it. I don't intend to have a daughter of mine spend the rest of her life singing hymns and praying to some character off in never-never land.

ART: *(Startled)* You mean Jan has got religion?

FATH: Not only that — she's evidently got your mother going back to that — that — opiate of the masses.

MOTH: Jim, it's called faith.

FATH: *(As if it were a dirty word)* FAITH!

MOTH: Yes, faith. This opiate, as you call it, has changed Janice, yes! But a change so wonderful that even you will have to wonder at it. She's no longer lonely, afraid, and mixed up! This Jesus whom you know only as a word to be taken in blasphemy, has become someone in her life that we could never be. She's known mostly indifference, cursing, bickering, and a great deal of cruelty from you and me. Now, God has reached down through the love of a godly teacher who cared and has delivered Janice from all the harm we have done her these many years. Because Jesus Christ is real to her as her Savior, she now has meaning and purpose in her life. And because of her experience, I, too, have broken the chains with which you have bound me these years. Now, I am free! And Jim — I will not allow you to touch Janice with your venom again!

FATH: Well — aren't you the brave one? Listen! If you and Janice want to wallow in all your guilt complexes, I won't stand in your way! *(He turns to go)* Right now I'm going back down with the boys. *(He storms out)*

ART: *(Looking at his mother for a moment)* I gotta admit it — whatever this is, it's sure made a change in you, mother. *(He leaves.)* *(Mrs. Marsten stands for a moment, looking after him, then kneels to pick up the pieces of the torn letter.)*
(Curtain)

Scene V

NAR: It is December, and Janice is home for the Christmas holidays. For the first time since September, the Marsten family is together. Although the household is somewhat divided, there has been no outward explosion. It is now dinner time on Christmas Day. Mr. Marsten, Arthur, and Janice have already been seated, but Mrs. Marsten pauses a minute to exclaim —

MOTH: Well — this is our first Christmas dinner together in so many years. *(She sits)* It seems so good to have no one away on a trip, or sick — or something.

FATH: Well, I'm hungry. Let's eat and forget the speeches. *(He*

84

reaches for food as Janice and mother bow their heads. Arthur also begins to reach for food, but seeing his mother and sister with bowed heads, he draws back his hand and looks at his father and waits quietly until they are through.)

JAN: *(With feeling)* It's been a wonderful Christmas!

ART: Yeah! There hasn't been one battle — yet!

MOTH: *(Gently)* Arthur!

FATH: *(Waving his fork and talking with his mouth full)* He's right! I guess it must be your good influence, Janice.

JAN: Thanks, dad, but I believe it's the spirit of Christmas. And speaking of Christmas — I can't get over what a terrific present that record player is, dad.

ART: I'll say it is! What made you think of getting Janice that?

JAN: The girls will sure envy me.

FATH: Oh, it wasn't anything really. There are plenty more where that one came from.

(There is a strange silence.)

JAN: What do you mean, daddy? Where did it come from?

FATH: Now don't start looking a gift horse in the mouth! The company will never miss it, and you'll get a lot of pleasure from it.

JAN: You mean to say that you stole my Christmas present?

FATH: No, I didn't steal it — I just — Look, we have dozens of these just lying around the plant. We give them away to salesmen and buyers as premiums. We help ourselves once in a while, and nobody cares. You never asked questions before about the little gifts I've always brought home. Why all the concern now?

JAN: But, daddy! With your income you could just as easily have bought it! A Christmas gift is supposed to be yours to give. And buying it makes it yours TO give.

FATH: *(Getting angry)* Oh, all right! So I'll pay for it when I go back to work after the holiday.

MOTH: I think that's wonderful, Jim.

FATH: *(Flaring up)* Oh, you do. Well, I don't! You're making me look like a common thief, and I don't like it. It looks like your holy, holy, holy attitude is going to be as difficult to live with as your stupid nagging.

JAN: Oh, daddy, it's been so nice at home up to this point. Let's not spoil it with an argument!

ART: Yeah—I kinda like it around home when it's peaceful and quiet!

FATH: *(Turning on Arthur)* So you're becoming one of them too, are you? The whole lot of you — ganging up on me!

ART: I'm not siding with anyone, dad. I was only making an observation!

FATH: Well, it still makes me out to be the big bad wolf. For two cents I'd leave this happy domestic scene and go somewhere

85

where a man is accepted for what he is and not have to be made over into something else.

(Arthur calmly tosses two pennies in front of his father's plate. Mr. Marsten glares for a moment, is about to say something, then slams down his fork and stalks out.)

JAN: *(Reprovingly)* Arthur! Was that necessary?

ART: *(Slowly and with confidence)* Aw — he'll be back. I think he likes the change around here. Only he doesn't want to admit it.

JAN: You really think so? *(Turning to mother)* Wouldn't it be wonderful if we really became a family, mother?

MOTH: Your father is a very stubborn man, Janice.

JAN: Art, you said you thought daddy liked "the change" as you call it. How about you?

ART: *(After a moment of silence he turns to his mother.)* Mother, I have a confession to make. I saw you reading those letters from Janice, and I sneaked in and read them too. *(Turning to Janice)* Tell me straight, Jan, did all this change in you really come as a result of your learning about — about —

JAN: Go ahead, Art, say it.

ART: Did *Jesus Christ* make all the difference?

JAN: Yes, Art. He has changed my whole life.

ART: *(Rather self-consciously)* Well, mother, remember that sort of run-in we had with Michael Brandt a month or so ago, about Darwin's theory as against the creation story? He really shook me up, and I was sure angry. But when we threw him out of the club, he never held it against us at all! That really started me thinking, because I know how I'd have reacted if I'd been tossed out! *(Arthur turns to Janice)* Then when I got curious about those letters that mother was reading, and they seemed to — all of a sudden — make a change in her, I sneaked in and read them without mother knowing I had. All the things you said in your letters — and the change it's made in you and mother! Well, it just seems like a miracle!

JAN: Salvation *is* a miracle, Art.

ART: *(Uncomfortably, but with determination)* Jan, — I'd like to know about — your Jesus!

JAN: *(After looking at her mother, she lays a hand on Arthur's arm.)* Art, He's not just mine! He belongs to all who will believe.

ART: Will you tell me about Him?

JAN: Yes, Art. I'll tell you as much as you want to know. He's a wonderful Person to know.

ART: *(To his mother)* There's something about this that seems to have affected dad, too. Have you noticed that he hasn't come into the house with liquor on his breath for over a week?

MOTH: Yes, son — I've noticed.

(Curtain)

NAR: So it was that the Marsten family came face to face with Jesus Christ. A faithful messenger presented the path of faith to one member, and the tiny flame she ignited in that heart became a torch of faith that illuminated a household!

THE LOST SON

A dramatic interpretation of Christ's
parable from Luke 15:11-24.

Dramatizing the Scriptures is a task that demands of the author
not only the skills of the performing arts, but a more than casual
knowledge of the theology involved. Authors attempting to dramatize
the eternal truths of God's Word without an intimate relationship with
God invariably do violence not only to the text, but to the intent
of the Author of those Scriptures, the Holy Spirit.

I believe that sacred drama, created for and dedicated to the purpose of rightly dividing the Word of Truth, can prepare hearts for
that moment when Christ calls. I offer this drama, "The Lost Son,"
with the prayerful hope that its content may be used of God to propa-
gate the faith and to bring encouragement to the faithful.

Instructions

To achieve the most effective results, two areas of action would be
best. The main acting area may be the usual proscenium stage with
curtain, scenery, and lighting.

The secondary area of action is of simple design. The most efficient
proceduce would be to construct a small jury stage to the left or right
of the proscenium so that the three actors upon it are readily seen by
the audience and can be blacked out as the action shifts to the main
stage. An area 8' by 10' will suffice (see Fig. 1).

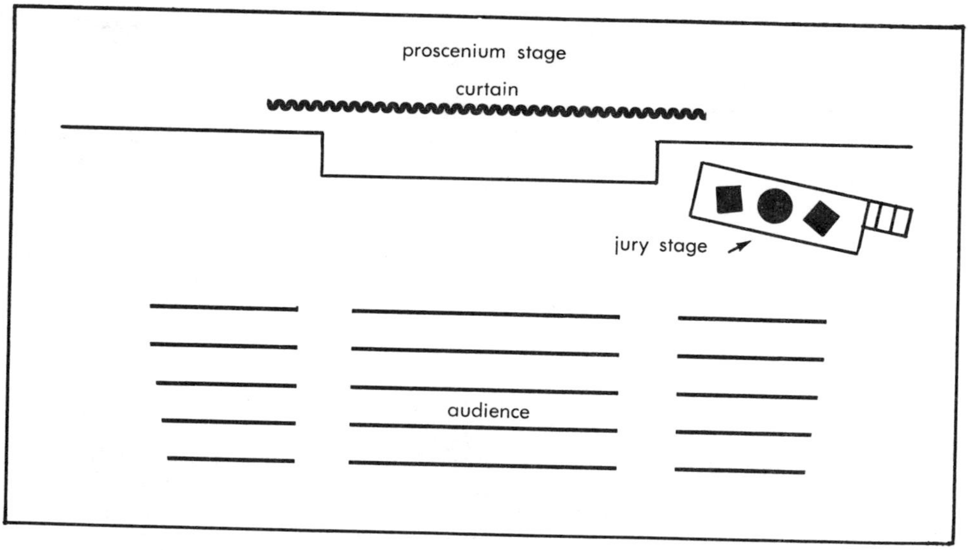

fig. 1

The two stages are used in this fashion. The proscenium stage carries all the action of the drama dealing with the activities of the son. The scenery is set up during the time when the action shifts to the jury stage.

If traditional flats and properties are used, the scenes must be simple and adapted to quick, noiseless changes. Effective results may be realized by utilizing a nearly bare stage, with just enough properties to simulate the different localities. Imaginative lighting, highlighting the areas of action, is very rewarding. However, the traditional settings with flats, cyclorama and properties offer the most challenging vehicle for this particular effort.

The jury stage may be as ambitious or efficient as time and space will permit. If scenery to create the effect of a corner of a living room is available, a very attractive production is possible.

The basic properties include a large easy chair for the father, an attractive lamp for lighting, and two pillows on which the two children sit. The background may be a bookcase or a window setting. Should one wish to have the mother appear, in place of her being but a voice, a flat with a practical doorway can be used, although her part is so small it will not add appreciably to the drama.

Characters on the Secondary Stage

Mr. Carlson - father
Brad Carlson - son, about nine
Marla Carlson - daughter, about eleven
Mrs. Carlson - mother

Characters in the Drama

Roger - prodigal son, about eighteen
Paul - his brother, about twenty-one
Father - about forty
Messenger
Ralph - Roger's friend, about thirty
Rita - girl friend, about thirty
Landlady
Overseer
Worker
Foreman

THE DRAMA

As the lights come up on the secondary stage, the proscenium curtain is closed. The lights reveal a living room in the Carlson home. Two children are seated on the floor, one on either side of a chair in which Mr. Carlson is seated, Marla, seated, to the right of the big chair, and Brad, seated to the left, have been listening to their father read from the Bible and have enjoyed a story which he has just finished. Mrs. Carlson is in the kitchen, offstage, Mr. Carlson is speaking.

89

MR. C: You come up with the strangest requests, Brad. This one tops them all! You want me to tell you the story of a boy who fed pigs?

BRAD: *(Eagerly)* Yes, daddy . . . . don't you remember it?

MR. C: Oh . . . . I've told it before?

BRAD: Yup! A long time ago. *(Thoughtfully)* All I can remember is that he was very rich and he wanted to feed pigs!

MR. C: *(Amused)* That's a help. He was rich and wanted to feed pigs. That *really* sets him apart from the usual, I must say, but I can't seem to remem . . . . .

MARLA: *(Suddenly interrupting)* Brad's right, daddy! I remember now. There *was* a boy who fed pigs.

MR. C: Well! We're getting *somewhere,* now two down and me to go.

MARLA: You *must* remember, daddy. He ran away from home and when he came back his father was so glad to see him, he gave him a ring and cooked a great big dinner!

MR. C: *(In mock seriousness)* Wait a minute! I'm getting an idea. If you just give me another clue or two, perhaps I can . . . .

BRAD: *(Suddenly)* I remember now! He lost all his money in the stock market and decided to feed pigs!

MR. C: That's the clue! You mean the prodigal son!

MARLA: That's the one! The Lost Son!

BRAD: And he fed pigs!

MARLA: Didn't he inherit a lot of money and then lose it all?

BRAD: *(Trying to interrupt)* And he fed pigs.

MR. C: That's partly true, Marla. Actually he . . .

BRAD: *(Trying to interrupt)* And he fed pigs.

MR. C: *(Continuing)* . . . didn't inherit the money . . . he asked if he might have his portion of his father's estate to do with as he pleased.

BRAD: *(Still trying)* And he fed pigs.

MR. C: Then he left home and spent his portion very foolishly.

BRAD: Buying food for pigs.

MR. C: *(Finally noticing Brad)* What did you say, Brad?

BRAD: He lost all his money in the stock market and buying food for pigs!

MARLA: *(Impatiently)* Oh, Brad! He didn't lose his money in the stock market . . . he spent it foolishly.

BRAD: I know . . . buying food for pigs.

MARLA: *(Still a bit impatiently)* No! He lost his money by spending it all on having a good time. When it was all gone, he had to have a job, so he . . .

MR. C: *(Interrupting)* Wait a minute, Marla. I thought you wanted *me* to tell the story?

MOTHER: *(From the kitchen offstage)* Ralph . . . it's about bedtime.

Finish the story you're telling and send them upstairs to brush
their teeth and get ready for bed.

MARLA: *(Softly and hurriedly)* Quick, daddy . . . start the story before you answer mother, so we can stay up a while longer . . .
hurry, daddy!

MR. C: *(Softly)* You know I can't do that, Marla!

MOTHER: Did you hear me, Ralph?

MARLA: *(Pleading)* Oh, please, daddy!

MR. C: *(Undecided, then quickly and softly)* All right, but just this
once! *(Rapidly)* Once-upon-a-time-there-was-a-boy-who-fed-pigs!
(Then loudly, to the kitchen) I heard you, dear. We'll just finish
this story and then off to bed!

MOTHER: All right, Ralph.

MARLA: *(Giving her father a big hug)* Oh, daddy . . . you're just the
best daddy in the whole world. Isn't he, Brad?

BRAD: *(Thinking very deeply)* Is that the way the story began?

MR. C: *(Mussing Brad's hair)* Not exactly, deep thinker.

BRAD: Start from the beginning, daddy, and when you come to the
part where he feeds the pigs, be sure and go real slow so I won't
forget this time.

MR. C: All right, son. Now . . . let's see . . . it all began way back . . .

BRAD: *(Interrupting)* Daddy?

MR. C: Yes, Brad.

BRAD: Are you going to tell it like it was way back in the time of
Jesus?

MR. C: Why?

BRAD: I was just thinking . . . couldn't you tell this one like you did
the one about the good Samaritan?

MR. C: You mean, as if it happened just yesterday?

MARLA: That's a good idea, daddy, just as if it happened yesterday.
I like it when you do it *that* way.

BRAD: *(Excitedly)* And maybe he could take a jet, or a nuclear sub-
marine, or . . .

MR. C: Whoa-a-a, there! Let's not get carried away! Jesus told a
very simple story to demonstrate a truth. I'm not sure we should
add too much to it.

BRAD: Aw-w-w . . . I don't think He'd mind. Anyway, I think the
copyright has run out.

MR. C: *(Laughing)* Copyright? What do you know about copyrights?

MARLA: Don't you remember, daddy? Last week we were looking
through a book from the library and . . .

BRAD: And I asked you what the word "copyright" meant. Remember? It was at the bottom of a page and you said it meant that . . .

MR. C: *(Stopping him)* All right . . . I remember. But Jesus' stories
are different. His parables aren't copyrighted.

BRAD: *(Vehemently)* Oh yes they are!

MR. C: What?

BRAD: It says so right in the Bible. (*He reaches over and turns to the front of the Bible on Mr. Carlson's lap.*) Right there! See?

MR. C: (*Looking*) Well . . . it certainly says "copyrighted" doesn't it?

BRAD: (*Wisely*) But it must have run out by now, hasn't it, daddy?

MR. C: (*In mock seriousness*) I should think so, after 2,000 years.

MARLA: Oh, daddy, you aren't agreeing with him, are you?

MR. C: Look for yourself, Marla. (*Shows her the Bible*) It says right there, "Copyrighted, 1959."

MARLA: But it also says that it refers to the special helps and references, and things like that . . . things that are put there to help us better understand and . . . (*Looks at Mr. Carlson*) Oh, daddy . . . you're just teasing. You knew that!

MR. C: (*Smiling*) Perhaps I did, but I bet Brad will always remember that the Bible belongs to everyone . . . and that its truths are free and no one can copyright any part of God's Word. Right, Brad?

BRAD: Right, daddy! No copyrights . . . no royalties . . . no nothing!

MARLA: Let's have our story before mother thinks we're stalling.

MR. C: Right!

BRAD: Remember, daddy . . . just like it happened yesterday.

MR. C: All right. Now . . . where shall we say the story began?

BRAD: (*Thinking quickly*) I know . . . make him a cowboy. I like cowboys!

MR. C: That sounds like a good idea. Okay, Marla?

MARLA: Sure. I like horses!

MR. C: Then we'll say that they all live on a big ranch in Texas. Here's how it all began. A big rancher had two sons.

BRAD: One older than the other.

MR. C: That seems logical.

MARLA: Stop interrupting, Brad.

MR. C: One day the two brothers were sitting in the living rcom of their big ranch house. The older brother was very busy working on books and ledgers. The younger brother was also busy, but he was looking at travel folders.

(*The curtain opens on the proscenium stage and the lights fade on the secondary stage at the same time. This is timed to coincide with the words "looking at travel folders."*)
(*The scene is the living room of the ranch house belonging to a very wealthy and successful cattleman.*)

ROG: Will you look at this! (*He thrusts a travel folder under the older son's nose.*)

PAUL: (*Completely engrossed in the ledgers*) Uh, uh.

ROG: Aw-w-w come on, fella . . . you didn't even look at it!

PAUL: Can't you see that I'm busy?

Rog: And can't you forget for just one evening that you're an heir to the largest ranch in the country? Put away the ledgers and relax! They'll be there in the morning. All work and no play . . . you know.

Paul: There's a time to relax and a time to work. Right now these records have to be kept. I'd suggest you put in a few moments of real work and stop daydreaming over those travel folders.

Rog: Oh . . . it's all right for you to bury your nose in those ledgers and cattleman's journals . . . but for me? I'm planning to shuck this whole rat race and go see the world while I'm still young enough to enjoy it. If you want to drag your feet and grow roots here, go ahead! Count cattle all your life! Give me the chance and I'll snap it up *(snaps finger)* just like that!

Paul: And while you're out "Seeing The World" who will do your work here at the ranch?

Rog: And I've got that all figured out, too!

Paul: Oh?

Rog: Yes-sir-ree! When dad gets back from this trip I'm going to say, dad . . . .

Father: *(From the doorway)* Did I hear my name?

Paul: *(Jumping up)* Father . . . you're back early!

Rog: *(Flustered)* We . . . that is . . . well . . . we didn't expect you back 'til tomorrow.

Father: *(Smiling)* So I gathered. *(Pause)* Well?

Rog: Well . . . what, dad?

Father: I believe you were about to deliver a speech to me.

Rog: *(Momentarily embarrassed)* Oh . . . that. I'd really planned to pick my own time for *that* one.

Father: Planned?

Rog: Well . . . yes! But, as long as you know I have a speech prepared, I guess now is as good a time as any. *(Deliberately)* Dad . . . you said that one day I'd inherit a portion of the ranch. You said I could do with it as I pleased. Well . . . I think that right now I could put my share to better use than here at the ranch. As long as it will come to me ultimately, anyhow, I'd like my portion now, so I can invest it elsewhere. I think that now, while I'm still young, is a good time to make my own way. I'd like to see the world, too, and I can't do that tied down to the ranch. *(Paul sits down slowly, unbelief on his face.)*

Father: *(Looking at Roger for a long moment in silence)* Son . . . I've seen this unrest growing in you for a long time. I was hoping you would perhaps . . . . You've made up your mind to this, then?

Rog: Yes, father, I have.

Father: All right, son . . . if this is what you want.

Paul: *(Rising from his chair)* But father . . . divide the ranch now?

93

FATHER: *(Turning to him)* Patience, son! I've brought both of you to manhood, allowing you to make your own way as much as possible. This is your brother's decision. You have the same freedom. Would you deny *him* his birthright?

PAUL: *(Sitting slowly)* No . . . you're right, father. I will accept your decision.

FATHER: *(Turning to Roger)* Then it's all settled. If this is what you want, son, I'll have the lawyer come out tomorrow and . . . .

ROG: *(Rushes over to his father)* Boy, dad, that's great! Just great! And you won't be sorry! You'll see! I've got some great plans! You'll be proud of me! *(Starts for the door and then turns)* When I come back, I'll drive up to the front door in a big, white Cadillac! *(Spreading his arms wide)* The whole world is mine and . . . *(Suddenly quiet)* . . . wait 'til the fellas at the club hear this! Wow! *(Exits)*

(The father stands for a long moment, looking after his son. The curtain closes. As the curtain closes, the lights come up on the secondary stage.)

MR. C: *(As if continuing the story)* So the big day arrived and the younger son . . .

BRAD: *(Interrupting)* Dad!

MR. C: Yes, Brad.

BRAD: How could they divide the ranch? He couldn't take it with him, could he?

MARLA: Oh, Brad . . . you can come up with the funniest questions!

MR. C: No, Marla . . . it's a good question. How would you answer it?

MARLA: It's very simple . . . the father just asked the lawyer to . . . to . . . well . . . *(Finally)* I don't know, daddy, how did they divide it?

MR. C: *(Laughing)* Jesus didn't say exactly how it was done, but perhaps they did something like this. They figured how much all the property was worth, divided it equally, in terms of money, and gave one share to the younger son.

BRAD: Wow! That ranch must have been worth a million dollars!

MR. C: We're forgetting one thing.

BRAD: What's that?

MR. C: How do you suppose his father felt?

MARLA: Oh . . . we *did* forget that, didn't we? *(Sadly)* I should think he'd be very sad.

BRAD: I don't! He made his son real happy, didn't he? And daddy, you always ask us if we're happy after something nice happens, and when we say "yes," you always say, "Well, then . . . I'm happy." So . . . his daddy must have been happy too!

MR. C: That makes a pretty solid argument, Brad, but I'm afraid this is just a bit different.

94

BRAD: You mean his father wasn't happy?

MR. C: I think I'll let you answer that, Brad. Now . . . let's suppose that I take you down to our factory and teach you all about making boxes.

BRAD: *(Excitedly)* You told me you were going to do that when I was older, because someday I'd own our factory. When do we start? Am I old enough now?

MARLA: *(Impatiently)* Oh, Brad . . . Daddy's only making a "for-instance!"

BRAD: He did so tell me he'd teach me all about making boxes, and that someday I'd own the factory and run it! Didn't you, daddy?

MR. C: That's true, but right now I'm making a "for-instance" just as Marla said.

BRAD: *(Pause)* Oh! Okay, daddy, I understand. Sort of a "let's pretend" story to make something plain to me.

MR. C: That's right, Brad. So . . . you learn all about making boxes and soon you are superintendent.

BRAD: Like Mr. Nelson?

MR. C: Just like Mr. Nelson. I'm real proud of you and I'm making many wonderful plans so I can turn over the whole factory to you someday. Then one day you come to me and say, "Daddy . . . I don't want to make boxes all my life. I want to go out and see the world and make my living somewhere else. Give me my share of the factory now and I'll invest it." How do you think I'd feel, Brad?

BRAD: I guess you'd feel real bad, daddy. But I'd never do anything like that!

MR. C: Well . . . . that's what this young man did. *(Slowly)* You know, Marla and Brad, that's just the way some people treat God.

MARLA: They do? How do you mean, daddy?

MR. C: They accept all the good things that God offers . . . health, nice home, love, salvation . . . then they say to him, "God . . . I want to live my own way. I'm going to take all this that You've given me and spend it my way. I don't want to live the way You ask me to. It's too confining. I want to enjoy life my way, not Your way!"

MARLA: *(Thoughtfully)* Then Jesus was using a parable to illustrate.

MR. C: That's right, Marla. Jesus was showing us that, just as the son rewarded his father with ingratitude and selfish independence, so many people reward their heavenly Father by using the very things that He gives them to draw further away from Him.

BRAD: I don't understand, daddy.

MR. C: Think about it, Brad. We'll go back to you as superintendent of our factory. You want your share of the factory so that you can leave home and invest it elsewhere. Without me there wouldn't

95

be any factory for you to divide . . . . and without that share, you couldn't leave or have your share to invest elsewhere.

BRAD: *(Suddenly seeing it all)* I see it now, daddy! People use the very things God gives them to get away from Him.

MR. C: That's it, Brad. Isn't it strange? People cannot speak a word or breathe a breath against God without the very breath that God gives them . . . yet, God loves us, even as the rancher loved his wayward son.

MARLA: You make it all sound so . . . well . . . so . . . real, daddy!

BRAD: *(Very seriously)* I think we understand enough about this, daddy. Let's get to where he goes to work on a pig ranch.

MARLA: It's not a pig ranch . . . it's a pig farm! And a lot happens to him before that, anyhow.

MR. C: *(Laughing)* All right . . . we'll get to the . . . "pig ranch, or farm" whichever the case may be. *(Picks up Bible)* It says here that ". . . not many days after, the younger son gathered together, and took his journey into a far country and there wasted his substance in riotous living. And when he had spent all, there arose a famine in the land, and he began to be in want."

BRAD: What's substance, daddy?

MR. C: That means his money, or whatever his money could buy.

BRAD: And now he hasn't any money left?

MR. C: Right. All his father gave him is gone. He sits alone in his room . . . his pocket and his heart are empty. His latest financial venture is doomed to fail because of the drought that is in the land. Right now he's awaiting a visit from one of his friends whom he sent for . . .

(The proscenium curtain opens and the secondary lights fade as Mr. Carlson says . . .)

and from whom he hopes to borrow enough to recover his losses. *(The scene reveals Roger seated at a table. It is piled high with papers and ledgers. The room is very tastefully furnished and is in what appears to be a fashionable apartment. There is a knock on the door.)*

ROG: Yes . . . yes . . . come in . . . come in!

MESSEN: *(Opening the door and coming up to the table)* I have a message from your foreman, sir.

ROG: *(Reaching for it)* Let me have it. *(Messenger hands him the note and Roger reads)* "What I said in the last message is true. The drought has wiped out your crops and threatens the cattle and horses. The famine is very severe. Unless you can raise the money, or feed in the quantity I stipulated in my last letter, your creditors will claim what is left of your holdings. Unless I hear from you by tomorrow, I shall consider myself free and seek work elsewhere. I promised the bearer of this message that you would pay him for delivering it to you. Please accept my. . . . *(The son*

96

crumples the paper savagely.) I can't believe it! It's all gone! With just a little rain . . . .

MESSEN: Do you wish me to take a note back, sir?

ROG: *(Startled)* What? Oh . . . No . . . There's no need. Here . . . *(He hands him some coins)* . . . . this will repay you for your journey .

MESSEN: Thank you, sir *(Backing towards the door).* I hope things will turn out all right for you, sir.

ROG: Thank you. A safe journey home. *(Messenger exits)* *(Roger sits slowly in the chair. He slowly opens the crumpled paper and begins to read it again, then re-crumples it and tosses it into waste-basket. He gets up and paces back and forth.)* If only I hadn't put everything into that ranch! *(Looks at his watch)* What time is it? Ralph will be here any minute! He's my last chance to make things work out. *(Returns to table)* Let's see. . . . I'd better get these out of sight.

(He begins to stuff papers into a drawer)

RALPH: *(Suddenly appearing in the doorway with Rita.)* Well! Aren't you the busy one?

(Ralph and Rita enter)

Don't you know it's time to play, not work? *(To Rita)* Look, Rita . . . . he isn't dressed for the party yet.

RITA: *(Fingering papers on table)* Perhaps he prefers these papers to people! *(Shrill laugh)*

ROG: *(Still sorting papers)* All play and no work . . . . I do have to make a living, you know.

RALPH: No, I didn't know! The way you've been throwing money around, I thought your funds were unlimited!

RITA: *(Sarcastically)* And all the time he's actually been a *big tycoon!*

RALPH: I got your note about an hour ago. What's up? You sounded urgent.

ROG: *(Covering up)* Did I? It's not really urgent, but I'm glad you came, anyway.

RALPH: *(Indicating papers)* What's all this? Papers . . . . ledgers?

ROG: Just some business deals I'm preparing to close. That's why I asked you to come . . . . I need your advice.

RALPH: Business deals? *(Laughs)* Oh, come now! I can see you writing out a big check with a flourish . . . or handing a waiter a huge tip, but business! You a business man? All you know is fun, frolic and feasting! *(Picks up a paper or two)* Wait a minute . . . these look like . . . . *(looking at them)* . . . . why . . . they're bills, not contracts!

ROG: *(Grabbing for papers)* Here . . . . give me those . . . . you've no right . . . .

RALPH: *(Holding papers beyond Roger's reach)* Listen to this, Rita,

"Dear Sir: Unless we receive prompt payment, we will consider your account delinquent and closed."

RITA: *(Snatching another paper from table)* "Owing to your refusal to come in and see us about you overdue bill," . . . the *overdue* is underlined, "we have no recourse but to repossess."

RALPH: *(Looking at it and whistling)* Look at the amount on this one, Rita! *(Shows it to her)*

RITA: Wow-ee! That would buy a lot of trinkets!

RALPH: That's a pretty hefty sum, boy, but I can remember when you used to throw that much on the gaming table on the turn of a card, but I guess the odds have finally caught up with you . . . right?

ROG: You've no right to . . . .

RALPH: Don't tell me the highflying, big-time rancher has had his wings clipped. Is that why you called me over?

ROG: All right . . . . all right! So I'm a bit short for the moment.

RALPH: Short? Oh, come now . . . . admit it . . . . you're flat broke! It's all over town you've lost your shirt on that ranch. Are you trying to hide it from Ralphy Boy?

ROG: What if I am temporarily embarrassed? I'll make out all right. All I need is a small loan and a little time. That's why I asked you to come. *(Trying to sell his position)* I *know* cattle and I *know* horses. With a little help I can weather this little rough spot. I'll soon get my head above water, but I need some ready cash to tide me over. You know I'll be good for it and a modest loan is something you can easily afford.

RALPH: *(Leaning over table)* Hah! Are you serious? I warned you . . . we *all* warned you against trying to raise livestock in this area. There just isn't any assurance that there's enough water and workable soil to support such a venture. We also warned you that one of our drought years could wipe you out! But you thought you *knew* so much! Well . . . . here we are right in the middle of one of our droughts and what's worse, it's developed into quite a famine and you're *dead!* There's no pasture, no feed, no water, no *nothing!*

RITA: Tell him what he should have done, Ralph.

RALPH: Now . . . if you'd put your money, like the rest of us, into running guns for the Commies, you'd be sitting pretty. But, no! You said you still had scruples! Scruples? Tell me . . . where did you get all that money you've been throwing around, in the first place?

ROG: I didn't steal it if that's what you mean.

RALPH: It doesn't make any difference where it came from . . . everyone marked you for a hayseed, straight out of Hicksville, trying to act like a man-of-the-world, right from the very beginning. So now you're short of money and all you can think of is to borrow from one of us. Well . . . we've all been through lean days too, but we've managed to come out on top without running and begging from our friends . . . now it's your turn. This is a high-flying crowd you've been traveling with . . . but if you can't stand the altitude . . . turn in your oxygen mask. Loan you money? Not on your life! *(Turning to the door)* Come on, Rita . . . the gang's waiting. *(He takes her arm and leads her to the door, then turns)* By the way . . . . don't bother to drop around for any good-bys. I'll gladly spread the news of your . . . ah . . . shall we say . . . withdrawal from the clan! *(They exit laughing)*

RITA: *(As they are heard in the distance)* Turn in your oxygen mask! Oh, Ralph, you're a poet! *(Laughter fades)*
(Roger sinks dejectedly into the chair and puts his head in his arms. There is a gentle knocking at the door.)

LANDL.: *(Entering)* It's me, sir . . . . the landlady. May I come in?

ROG: *(Raising his head)* Yes . . . . come in.

LANDL.: Begging your pardon, sir . . . you told me to come in after your friends had left. I couldn't help overhearing what they said as they left. Are you really through with that crowd? If you are, sir, it's a good thing. They're a bad lot, *those* young ones.

ROG: So I discovered. *(Cautiously)* Did you hear everything?

LANDL.: Oh, no, sir! I heard them say something about your withdrawal, as they went out. *(Pause)* You asked me to come in after they were gone, sir. Do you have the money?

ROG: Oh . . . . yes . . . . the money. *(Pause)* I'm sorry.

LANDL.: Sorry? I don't understand, sir.

ROG: *(Imitating her)* "I don't understand, sir!" *(His own voice)* Here! *(Tosses a few coins on the table)* That's what I mean! I'm washed up! Wiped out!

LANDL.: You mean . . . what they said is true . . . you've no money at all?

ROG: So . . . you did hear it all! Well . . . then you know!

LANDL.: Then you've been stalling me all these months. All your talk about a *big* deal . . . and the *big* bonus you'd give me for my patience . . . all adds up to a *big* nothing! Well . . . my *big* heart is *big* fed up! Now, you clear out of here in ten minutes and take nothing but the clothes on your back or I'll sic my dogs on you!

ROG: *(As she turns to go, he says bitterly)* Wait! Haven't you forgotten something? *(He indicates the coins on the table)* Aren't you going to pick the bones clean?

LANDL.: *(Walking slowly toward him and spitting the words out)* Now you listen to me, you worthless young whelp! Don't talk to me about picking your bones clean! You've done that little job pretty well, all . . . by . . . your . . . self! You threw your money away as if it were going out of style! Parties . . . big cars . . . flashy clothes . . . and most of all, your stupid investments! Don't talk to me about picking any bones clean . . . you've done the job all by yourself . . . . Now get out!

ROG: *(Thoroughly deflated)* But . . . if you turn me out, I'll have nothing. Where will I go? What will I do?

LANDL.: That's really no concern of mine! You've been eating pretty high off the hog for some time now . . . perhaps this will sober you up a bit!

(Roger sinks slowly in the chair)

Speaking of hogs . . . you didn't sell out to the Commies and that's at least some small thing in your favor, so for that I'll give you one small bit of information . . . . There's a pig farm just outside of town and the owner is looking for someone to tend his herds. It's not much, but it ought to fit to a T.

(The landlady exits. Roger slowly buries his head in his arms as he sits, completely broken, at the table. He begins to sob uncontrollably as the curtain closes.)

(Lights up on secondary stage)

MR. C: ". . . and he began to be in want." What a transformation that was for the son. From a lot to a little, from much to nothing. This was certainly not the direction he had in mind when he left his father's home. *(Turning to Brad)* You can see he didn't have any money with which to buy food for pigs, Brad.

BRAD: *(In deep thought)* I wonder what kind of dogs she had.

MARLA: Oh, Brad . . . .

BRAD: Daddy? I remember now . . . he did go and work for the man who owned the pig farm.

MR. C: Right, son.

BRAD: *(Speaking very slowly)* I was just thinking . . . the man who owned the pigs seemed to be doing all right . . . . I wonder if the son had put all *his* money in pigs, do you suppose he would have been all right too?

MR. C: *(Chuckling)* He should have had you as his foreman, son.

MARLA: I don't care what he did . . . I feel sorry for him, daddy.

MR. C: I guess everyone who's ever read the parable has, Marla.

MARLA: Daddy, you said earlier in the story that a lot of people treat God the way the son treated his father. Does everyone who treats God that way have something bad happen to them like this?

MR. C: Marla, they asked the same thing of Job. Do you remember what happened to Job?

MARLA: You told us about Job a long time ago and I do remember, daddy.

MR. C: Of course Job was dealing with the question, "Should the innocent suffer?" In the case of the wayward son, he suffered because he had willfully sinned.

100

BRAD: *(Wide-eyed)* Boy, daddy . . . does that mean if I sin big enough God will make me feed pigs?

MR. C: *(Patiently)* Not exactly, Brad. I don't believe that God either adds up our sins, or measures them. At least not to the point where He would decide that "That's it! You've sinned so much, that now you will have to feed pigs to pay for them!"

MARLA: Why not, daddy? The son sinned and because of his sin, he had to feed pigs. Isn't that what the story says?

BRAD: Yes, daddy . . . isn't that true?

MR. C: I agree with you, that as a result of the son's actions, he did end up feeding pigs, but there's something else too.

MARLA: Your "something elses" are always real interesting, daddy. Tell us.

MR. C: First each one of you has to answer a question. First, Marla. Remember the museum we went to last week? What great man did you see?

MARLA: *(Thinking)* Ah . . . . Abraham Lincoln. *(Quickly)* Only it wasn't Abraham Lincoln. It was only a make-believe person.

MR. C: Make-believe? But didn't he move and talk and stand up and breathe?

MARLA: Well . . . . yes, but it was all done with motors and tape recorders.

MR. C: Remember how they let you touch him? Didn't his skin feel real?

MARLA: Yes, but he was still just make-believe. He wasn't really alive.

MR. C: That's what I wanted you to say. He wasn't alive. Now, remember that while I ask Brad a question. *(Turning to Brad)* Brad, I'm sure you remember the time at the convention when you saw all those beautiful apples and bananas and grapes and a lot of other fruit set on the big table in the center of the hall. Do you?

BRAD: I sure do, daddy. You told me not to touch them.

MR. C: But you did touch them, didn't you?

BRAD: *(Sheepishly)* I ate one of the grapes.

MR. C: You *tried* to eat it, right?

BRAD: Only it wasn't real. I tried to chew it and it was made of plaster!

MR. C: Remember how you spat it out? But . . . why did you try to eat it?

BRAD: It looked real. I thought it was a real grape.

MR. C: So, what do we have? An Abraham Lincoln who wasn't alive, and a table full of fruit that wasn't real. They both looked like the real thing, but each was made from dead things . . . and no matter how attractive and alive they appeared, they were both a lie. This is what happened to the son. His father tried to tell him that near him, sharing his love and the comforts and

101

security of the ranch, was the real and true life. But the son saw the world apart from the ranch as a very attractive, desirable place to be.

MARLA: But he found it much different, didn't he, daddy?

MR. C: He certainly did. At home with his father, he could spend what he had and his father would always have more to give him. But when he left the ranch and his father's presence, when all he had was gone, there was no father to provide more. Then when he turned to his friends he found out that they . . . .

BRAD: *(Interrupting loudly)* I know what they were, daddy! They were "fair-weather" friends. You see . . . I remember that!

MR. C: You certainly did, Brad. Just as the son found that his friends of the world weren't real friends, so do those who turn away from God and seek just the pleasures and joys of the world find that there is no real *life* there.

MARLA: That's right, daddy. Jesus said that *He* was the Way, the Truth and the *Life*.

MR. C: So I'm afraid the son found that there was no real life or joy apart from his father. He found that it was all a lie. What promised to be a "high summer" of constant delight, turned out to be a "winter" of constant despair! Gone was his brash confidence, his worldly wisdom, his superior knowledge in regard to what was best for him. Rushing in to take their place were only disillusionment, defeat and despair!

BRAD: Those are big words, daddy, but I think I know what they mean.

MR. C: I'm sure you do, Brad. The son soon found out that which every follower of Christ discovers . . . . the world's blessings, when enjoyed within the love and disciplines of our heavenly Father, are rich and rewarding. When used apart from God's will, they become an imitation of life and Satan uses them to destroy the foolish!

BRAD: What happened next, daddy?

MR. C: Well . . . Roger went out and got that job feeding pigs.

BRAD: Did the landlady recommend him for the job?

MARLA: You don't need a recommendation to feed pigs, Brad!

MR. C: Probably not, Marla. But you see, children, it wasn't so much that he was feeding pigs. It was the difference between what he had and what he ended up with that makes the story especially strong. Fine clothes, a beautiful apartment, the best of food, and independence came to an end and he dropped down, down, down the social ladder to complete humiliation. The Bible says, ". . . and he went and joined himself to a citizen of that country; and he sent him into the fields to feed swine." His folly was complete. In two giant steps, his life was completely altered. From security and service, to saloon and slop, to swine and swill! . . . What a drop!

102

Brad: You sound like a preacher, daddy. But I like it anyway!

Mr. C: I'm glad you do, Brad. Who knows what happened next?

Brad: I . . . kinda remember, but you tell it, daddy.

Mr. C: Well . . . he couldn't go down any further. He certainly had hit the bottom. So there was only one way to look, now. Can you tell me which way, Marla?

Marla: That's easy . . . *up!*

Mr. C: Right! He could only look up. Sometimes that's why God lets us go down so that the only way to look *is* up.

Brad: I don't understand, daddy. Didn't he have to look down to feed the pigs?

Marla: Oh, Brad! It's just a figure of speech!

Mr. C: Maybe if we continue the story, you'll see what we mean, Brad.

Brad: Okay.

Mr. C: Here he is, out in the field taking care of the pigs. (*The lights begin to fade on the secondary stage.*) It wasn't enough that he had to feed pigs, but the overseer was a very rough and belligerent man who always seemed to be angry.

(*The curtain opens on a scene out in a large field. Roger and another helper are gathering husks and loading them into a large wagon. The overseer is shouting at them.*)

O'seer: All right! Let's get this feed loaded! I can't wait all day!

Rog: (*Speaking as he lifts an armful into the wagon*) I'm working as fast as I can!

O'seer: Well, it's not fast enough. If you can't keep up, we'll get someone else to do your job. (*Overseer exits*)

Rog: (*To other worker*) If they'd give us food, we'd have strength enough to work harder.

Worker: You agreed to work just for the privilege of having shelter in their barn for the cold nights. They *said* they couldn't feed you.

Rog: Yes, but I thought there would be time to go into the village and beg for food after the work was finished. By the time I get in from the fields, others have been to the village before me and there are precious few crumbs left to be begged.

Worker: Why don't you try another village? Perhaps there is work and food there.

Rog: What's the use? This drought is widespread. Conditions wouldn't be any better. At least I have a warm barn in which to sleep and maybe things will get better (*He stops and looks at the husks in his hand*) I wonder . . . . the pigs eat these husks and seem to thrive on them . . . I wonder . . . .

Worker: I wouldn't try it. They'll just make you sick.

Rog: I suppose so. If they were worth anything to people, they certainly wouldn't be feeding them to pigs.

103

WORKER: *(Picking up jug)* I'm going to get water for the trip to the other field. I'll be right back.

ROG: *(Resignedly)* I'll be here! *(He works for a few moments, then looks around. He mutters to himself.)* He says they'll only make me sick . . . I wonder. *(He looks about for a moment to see if his fellow-worker is coming. He selects a husk and bites into it and immediately begins to choke. He falls to his knees and begins to sob.)* OH GOD . . . WHAT WILL BECOME OF ME?

WORKER: *(Returning, finds him sobbing)* Here, here! Get hold of yourself, man. Things are pretty rough and all that, but giving up isn't going to help! *(He notices the husk with a bite out of it)* So you didn't believe me. *(Shakes head)* Well, we all had to find out the hard way, I guess. *(He reaches down and tries to pull Roger up)* Come on, now . . . come out of it. We aren't the only ones in this mess, you know. There must be thousands just as hungry and cold and homeless. Now straighten up and get hold of yourself!

ROG: *(Suddenly quiet)* What? What did you say?

WORKER: I just reminded you to face things like a man.

ROG: No . . . . no . . . . not that. You said a word that sounded like . . .

WORKER: Oh, come now . . . . I said a lot of words like, hungry, cold and homeless and . . . .

ROG: *(Suddenly)* That's it! *(Almost shouting)* Oh, I'm a blind, stupid fool!

WORKER: Now, see here . . . . I didn't say any such thing!

ROG: I *know* you didn't! I did! I said it! You said one word . . . . "home!" . . . And for the first time in my life I know myself for what I really am! I'm a blind, stupid fool! Look at me. Here I am, ragged, hungry, cold . . . *miserable!* I'm sleeping in a barn with pigs! I've even tried to eat their food! All this, and I have a home! *(Suddenly quiet)* At least I pray God it's not too late!

WORKER: *(Thoroughly puzzled)* You're here . . . in this stinking hole . . . like this . . . and you have a home? I don't understand.

ROG: It's a long story. Why . . . it's a fact . . . my father is the wealthiest rancher in our part of the country! He has dozens of hired hands and they have all they want to eat and more . . . while here *I* am, starving!

WORKER: If what you say is true, what in the world are you doing here?

ROG: Don't you see? I had to come this far and sink this low to really see myself. And what I see makes me sick! *(He grabs his companion by both shoulders and fairly shouts at him)* But I'm going home! *(Now he turns and says out over the audience)* Home! What a wonderful word! *(Very quietly)* I don't know whether my father will even let me set foot on the ranch, after what I've done . . . but if I have to crawl on my face to him, I'm going to say . . . *"Father . . . I've sinned against you and heaven . . . and am not worthy to be called your son! Just let me live here as one of your hired hands!*

O'SEER: *(Appearing suddenly)* What are you two doing just standing there? Now you bend your backs or I'll run you off the farm! Do you hear me? *(The worker cringes and stoops to pick up husks)*

ROG: *(Standing tall and looking steadily at the overseer)* I wouldn't pick up another husk for you if my life depended on it! You know where I'm going? I'm going home. I'm leaving *you* to wallow in this filthy pigpen! *(Turns to other worker)* Why don't you come home with me? There's food and warm beds.

WORKER: Naw . . . he's your father, not mine. He wouldn't accept me.

ROG: My father has never turned anyone away. Come with me.

WORKER: No. I'm not going to stay here, though. I'm sure I can find something better than this filthy job. I'll finish out the day here and then leave. Maybe someday we'll meet again.

ROG: *(Shaking his hand)* Good luck! *(He exits as curtain closes)*
(Lights up on secondary stage.)

MR. C.: *(As if continuing the story)* . . . at last he was on his way back home.

BRAD: Daddy?

MR. C.: Yes, Brad.

BRAD: I think I know, now, what you meant about looking up.

MR. C.: Oh?

BRAD: It's when people try to solve problems all kinds of ways until they finally get so deep that there's only one thing left to do . . . pray. And to pray you sorta look up to God!

MR. C.: That's right, Brad. I'm proud of you. Did you think of that while I was telling that part of the story?

BRAD: Not exactly, daddy. I remember when you told us that one other time.

MR. C.: And you remembered it, finally. And all along I thought only your sister had an IBM machine for a brain!

MARLA: Daddy . . . I guess the son was real happy, now that he was going home.

MR. C: Well . . . let's see if he was really happy. First he had to admit that he was wrong. Does it make you children happy to admit you are wrong?

BRAD: Not me!

MR. C.: Then . . . he'd have to face his friends. Pretty painful, don't you think? The ranch hands . . . his older brother . . . and of course his father. Do you still think he was very happy?

MARLA: I guess I used the wrong words, huh?

MR. C: Let's just say your *choice* of words leaves a little to be desired.

105

He did do one thing, though, that took a big load off his mind as he started home. Can you tell me what that was?

BRAD: *(Quickly)* I know . . . he wouldn't have to feed pigs anymore!

MR. C.: *(Laughing a bit)* That's pretty good thinking, Brad, but it was something a bit more profound than that, I think.

MARLA: If it's profound, *you'd* better tell us, daddy!

MR. C.: Maybe we can figure it out together. Shall we try?

BRAD: Sorta play detective, daddy?

MR. C: Yes . . . "sorta play detective." First clue . . . when he left home he turned his . . . his. . . .

BRAD: He turned all his toys over to his pals!

MR. C.: *(Chuckling)* That's not very profound, is it, Brad?

MARLA: He turned all his money into Traveler's Checks! That's profound!

MR. C.: Well . . . it may be, but it's not the answer we're looking for. I'll rephrase it. . . . To walk away from his home he had to turn his b . . . b. . . .

MARLA: *(Shouting)* Back! He had to turn his back!

MR. C.: Right!

BRAD: Aw! That's not very profound!

MR. C.: Be patient, Brad, we'll get to the profound part. Now . . . when the son decided to return home . . . what did he do?

BRAD: He turned around and faced home.

MR. C.: What did he turn his back on, then?

BRAD: *(Dejectedly)* On feeding pigs! That still isn't profound!

MR. C.: Wait a minute, son, we're not finished. When people run away from God, what do they do?

MARLA: *(Triumphantly)* They turn their backs on Him!

MR. C.: Right! Now, think carefully . . . when they turn around and come back . . . what do we call it?

BRAD & MARLA: *(Together)* Repent!

MR. C.: They *repent*. So . . . what did the son do?

MARLA: He repented!

MR. C.: Brad . . . can you tell me what it means to repent?

BRAD: It means to be sorry for what you've done.

MR. C.: And one more thing.

BRAD: *(Thinking)* Isn't that enough, daddy?

MR. C.: Just being sorry doesn't prove too much. Remember the pickpocket the police arrested so many times . . . we read it in the paper last week.

BRAD: I remember, daddy. He'd go to jail and when he got out, he'd steal again and go right back to jail again.

MR. C.: Each time he was caught, he told the judge he was sorry, didn't he? Actually he was only sorry that he'd been caught. He wasn't sorry for what he'd done. But . . . if he said he was sorry for what he'd done, then didn't pick any more pockets . . .

or . . . *turn his back on picking pockets,* he would then have *repented.*

MARLA: *(Very excited)* Now I see it, daddy! The son was sorry for what he'd done . . . and he stopped running away from his father . . . and he turned his back on what he'd been doing and was on his way back to ask his father to forgive him! Right, daddy?

MR. C.: Exactly! Repentance is turning around and doing just the opposite of what you've been doing wrong. That's just what the son did . . . he admitted he was wrong, he turned away from it and hurried home to ask his father to forgive him. So you see . . . his journey wasn't exactly a happy one, but a great load was off his mind, because he finally had come to himself and realized he'd been wrong all the time. It's a good thing to remember that a repentant heart is a heart filled with a wonderful peace.

BRAD: Hey! We can't leave him out on the road. Let's get him home so his daddy can give him that beautiful ring!

MR. C.: Now there's a practical reason. All right . . . he's on the road home. I'll tell you what we'll do. We'll leap the miles and get inside his father's home in advance of his arrival. His father is in the living room of the great ranch house discussing the work of the day. The years have come and gone, but not a day has gone by without his glancing out of the window and down the long, winding road leading to the ranch, hoping against hope for the sight of a familiar figure.

(Lights on the secondary stage fade during the last sentence. The proscenium curtain opens on the living room of the ranch house. The father is talking to his foreman.)

NOTE: *Prepare the scenery drop for the road scene to follow this living room scene. This drop may be set to be lowered just in front of the properties of the living room so that no props will have to be moved. The lights will blackout for a few moments and then come on as soon as the drop is lowered in place. This should be timed to take place in about ten seconds.*

FATHER: . . . and we'll put the large herd into the south range next week and put the small herd into the pasture south of the old hay sheds.

FOREMAN: That should work out fine, sir. Your son will be bringing in the new saddle stock tomorrow and we can put them right into the west corral and begin breaking them by Friday. *(The father looks out the window and suddenly stands motionless. The foreman notices his silence.)* What is it, sir?

FATHER: There's someone coming up the valley road.

FOREMAN: That must be the new hand for the Bar-B Ranch. He was expected today or tomorrow.

107

FATHER: But, wouldn't he be riding a horse?

FOREMAN: Yes . . . I suppose so. Let me look. (*Looking*) He's too far away to recognize, but it could be one of the neighbor's boys.

FATHER: No . . . can it be? Yes . . . it is . . . it's my boy! (*Excitedly*) Jim, it's Roger. He's come home! (*Quietly*) Quickly . . . hand me the binoculars. (*The foreman reaches for the binoculars in a cabinet near the window and hands them to the father. The father looks through the glasses.*)

FOREMAN: Is it really Roger, sir?

FATHER: Yes! Yes . . . it's Roger! (*Suddenly subdued*) Oh . . . look at him. He's so ragged and he looks so tired! Why . . . he can hardly walk! (*Handing glasses to the foreman*) I'm going out to meet him. (*He moves toward the door*) Tell Martha to draw a warm bath. Have her unlock Roger's room and set out some clean clothes! And Jim . . . sound the ranch bell to call in the hands! We're going to make this a *real* homecoming! (*As he pauses in the doorway*) And tell the cook I want to see him right away! (*He races out the door, his voice fading as he calls out*) Hurry, now . . . he'll soon be here!

FOREMAN: (*Moving over to the door and calling after him*) Yes, sir . . . I'll do it right away! (*Calling to stage right*) Martha! Come right away! Open up Roger's room! Hurry!
(*The foreman hurries offstage right as the lights fade to blackout. At the blackout, lower road drop. As soon as drop is in place, bring up lights on road scene.*)
(*The son enters from stage right. He walks slowly to about center stage and then stops as if looking out over the ranch buildings.*)

ROG: There's the row of silos . . . the big corral by the haysheds. They've built so many more! The house looks the same . . . (*He hears the bell being rung*) and there's the bell calling the hands in from the fields . . . someone's coming out the front door . . . it looks like . . . it is . . . father! But why is he running? He's going to close the gate so I can't come in! Oh, God . . . no! I want to come home! Please don't turn me away! . . . But he didn't stop at the gate! . . . He's running toward me!

FATHER: (*As if from the distance*) Roger! . . . (*Closer*) . . . Roger! . . . (*Very near*) . . . my son! (*The father hurries onto the stage and stops*) Roger! (*The son drops to his knees and bows his head. His father comes quickly and tries to kneel beside Roger.*) You've come home!

ROG: (*Attempting to push his father away*) Father . . . I have sinned against heaven and have dishonored your name! I don't ask you to take me back as your son . . . just give me a place to work on the ranch as a hired hand. Forgive me, father . . . I was wrong and I'm lonely and tired . . . don't turn me away. . . . I'm so ashamed and not worthy to be called your son!

FATHER: *(Kneeling down and grasping his son's shoulders)* Not worthy to be called my son? *(Folding him in his arms)* Oh my son . . . my son . . . my heart was breaking from sorrow when you left me . . . now I fear it will break from joy because you've returned! How I've prayed that you would come back to me . . . and now God has answered my prayers!

ROG: *(Looking into father's face)* Father . . . I have nothing left. I've wasted everything you gave me. I can never. . . .

FATHER: *(Stopping him)* Son . . . we'll speak no more of the years of separation. You've come back to me . . . that's all that matters! *(He stands and lifts his son to a standing position)* Here . . . let me look at you. Yes . . . your shoulders are broader, but you're so thin! Come, let's get rid of these worn clothes. You need a warm bath and a good meal under your belt. *(Starts to move offstage left.)*

ROG: Father?

FATHER: Yes, son?

ROG: Nothing, really. . . . I just wanted to see how it felt to say "Father" again. It's so good to be home!

FATHER: *(Pointing to left, over the audience)* Look, son . . . everyone's gathered at the house, waiting to welcome you home. They've all missed you, son. *(He shouts as if to those about the house)* What are you all standing about for? Martha . . . is Roger's room ready? Jim . . . Roger's clothes won't fit him anymore. Go up to my closet and bring down that new, brown suit of mine . . . and bring those new shoes down, also. *(He turns to Roger)* I see you're not wearing your favorite ring. Did you have to. . . .

ROG: Yes, father . . . I . . . I. . . .

FATHER: I know, son. . . . It was unkind of me to ask. *(He calls out again)* Joseph . . . hurry in and tell Jim that Roger lost the ring he always wore. Tell him to bring down the one on my dresser. . . . the one with the crest. *(To son again)* I want you to look as you always did . . . at your first meal at home. *(Suddenly)* No! Not just a meal . . . we'll have a banquet! *(Once again he shouts to those in the house)* Where's the cook? Oh . . . there you are! Cookie . . . I want you to go out in the barn and kill that calf we've been fattening up for the spring barbecue. I want you to fix all the trimmings! Martha . . . call up all the neighbors! Tell them Roger has come home and I want them to come and share in his homecoming! Tell them he isn't *dead* but is *alive!* Tell them he is no longer lost, but has been found! My son, Roger, has come back to me! Let everyone know that my son has come home! *(He turns to his son)* Welcome home, son.

(He folds him in his arms as the curtain closes.)

THE KING WHO CHOSE A BARN

A dramatic presentation of the events
related to the birth of Christ

Instructions
See Instructions for *The Lost Son*

Characters on the Secondary Stage
Mr. Carlson — father
Brad Carlson — son, about nine
Marla Carlson — a daughter, about eleven
Mrs. Carlson — mother

The Characters in the Drama

Characters in the Drama

Isaiah — the prophet
Ruth — Mary's friend
Mary — mother of Jesus
Gabriel — voice
Herod — king of Judea
Slave
Roman guards — I and II
Herod's ministers — I and II
Women of the Court — five or ten
Roman courier — young man
Joseph — Mary's husband
Merchant — Philius
Chief Priest
Priests — five or six

Balthazar — wise man
Melchior — wise man
Casper — wise man
Innkeeper
Innkeeper's wife
Shepherd boy — about ten
Shepherd — his father
Shepherds — five or ten
Shepherds — two who stay with
    sheep
Angel — voice
Angels — voices (choir)
Soloist — voice

The lights come up on the jury stage. Mr. Carlson is seated in a large chair with Brad on a pillow to his left, and Marla sitting on a pillow to his right. Behind him is a living room wall with a bookcase and pictures. A door leading out into the kitchen is to the left and behind them.
(If room will not permit a door, the voice of Mrs. Carlson can be heard from behind this scene, rather than having her come to the doorway.)
When the lights (or curtain opens) come up, Mr. Carlson is just closing a book as he speaks.

FATHER: That just about does it. You've had your story . . . and now it's time for you to say your prayers, kiss mother and daddy good night, and snuggle off to bed.

110

MARLA: Oh! Daddy! One doesn't snuggle off to bed! When you snuggle . . . it means . . . to . . . to . . . well, snuggle up close!

FATHER: That's what I said. . . . I want you both to go snuggle up real close to your pillows.

BRAD: *(Emphatically)* I'm not sleepy yet!

MARLA: Me neither! *(Impishly)* Maybe another story will be just enough to make us sleepy, daddy.

FATHER: *(Feigning sternness)* You're both a couple of fakers! Your eyes are so heavy, you can barely keep them open.

BRAD: *(Challenging)* Oh, no they're not! I'm awake as you are, daddy. See? *(Demonstrates)*

MARLA: And we can stay awake as long as you can, daddy.

BRAD: Let's see who can stay awake the longest!

FATHER: Oh, no you don't! You caught me with that once . . . not again!

MOTHER: *(Mother's voice is heard from backstage as if in other room)* Ralph . . . you may as well give them another story. Remember they both slept in the car coming back from Aunt Edna's this afternoon.

FATHER: I'd forgotten about that. Maybe that's a good idea.

MOTHER: Remember children. . . . Off to bed immediately after this story.

MARLA: We will, mother. Thanks!

BRAD: Yeah. . . . Thanks, mom!

FATHER: Wait a minute! I'm the one to thank, am I not? I'm telling the story!

MARLA: Shucks, daddy . . . we were just thanking mother for being the irresistible force that moved the movable object . . . you!

FATHER: That's not quite the way it goes . . . but I must admit . . . your mother is irresistible!

MOTHER: *(Coquettishly)* Why, Mr. Carlson . . . you say the nicest things.

FATHER: *(Turning back to the children)* All right . . . if it's a story . . . what kind shall it be?

BRAD: You pick one, daddy . . . you always pick good ones.

FATHER: *(Gazing upward in concentration)* Let's see, now . . . what shall I . . . I have it! Brad . . . where are kings born?

BRAD: That's easy . . . in castles.

FATHER: All right . . . now . . . what if I told you about a king who chose to be born in a barn?

BRAD: He did? Why did he choose a barn, dad? *(Suddenly)* Wait a minute! Babies don't choose!

FATHER: *(Chuckling)* That's right. I almost had you. But to tell you the truth . . . this one did choose. And what's more . . . he was named hundreds of years before he was born! So, you see . . . there's something special about this baby already.

111

BRAD: I'll say there is! But, I thought babies were named by their parents! How can... *(Noticing that Mr. Carlson is smiling a very special smile)* Oh-h-h-h! I see! You're giving me clues!

MARLA: Clues? What kind of clues?

BRAD: You know, Marla . . . like he does when he's teaching us something from the Bible. He always . . . *(Suddenly)* oh! . . . I know!

MARLA: *What* do you know, Brad?

BRAD: You're talking about Jesus!

FATHER: How do you know that?

BRAD: Well . . . He was a King and He was born in a stable . . . and that's kinda like a barn, isn't it?

MARLA: *(Suddenly)* And a prophet did say many years before He was born that He would be named Emmanuel!

FATHER: Very good. Now, why was He called Emmanuel?

MARLA: Because it means *"God With Us"* and Jesus was God, the Son, and He came to be *with* us on earth!

FATHER: Right on every count!

BRAD: Aw! that was easy! She read that in the Bible. *(Pause)* But, daddy . . . you said that Jesus *chose* to be born in a barn. How could a *baby* choose to be born in *any* place? Explain that away.

FATHER: Aren't you the skeptic? The Bible tells us that Jesus willingly came to lay down His life for all of us. He said, "I and the Father are one! So . . . if God knew way ahead when and where Jesus would be born . . . and Jesus and the Father are one . . . then . . . since God chose for Him to be born in a barn. . . .

MARLA: *(Suddenly)* Then, Jesus *did* choose to be born in a barn! See, Brad?

BRAD: *(Slowly)* I . . . guess . . . I . . . do. *(Not too sure)* Boy, daddy, it sounds so easy when you say it! What's next?

FATHER: Let's . . . see. . . . Have we named the prophet who told about Jesus' coming?

BRAD: Nope! That's easy. It was . . . I . . . I. . . .

MARLA: Isa. . . .

BRAD: *Don't* tell me, Marla . . . I know! It was . . . Isaiah!

FATHER: Good for you! Actually *many* prophets told of His coming. The important thing is that God started a *whole* series of events that happened *exactly* as the prophets, who prophesied, said they would. When you put them all together they're like an adventure story! Would you like to hear it?

BRAD: That would be *super*, daddy. Will it have a surprise ending like television?

FATHER: *(Laughing gently)* Well . . . not exactly, Brad. It did have a surprise or two for the Jews, I guess you could say, but all that the prophets spoke of came true, so there weren't any real surprises . . . except . . . except . . . *(He sees Brad perking up)* in a way there was a surprise ending.

MARLA: Really, daddy? A *real* surprise ending?

BRAD: *(Joyfully)* Oh boy! I knew it! I knew it! I figured there ought to be something besides just being born in a barn! I remember Reverend Olson talking about the *silent* years in Jesus' life. Is that where the surprise ending comes, daddy? I bet some rich person found Him and took Him home and bought Him a horse and a boat and a. . . .

FATHER: *(Interrupting)* Whoa! Wait a minute, son! Not that kind. It was a different sort of a surprise.

BRAD: Different? But . . . daddy . . . a surprise is a surprise, isn't it?

FATHER: Yes-s. . . . I suppose so . . . but this surprise was a long time coming and its surprise covered many years.

MARLA: How can a surprise cover many years, daddy?

BRAD: Yeah . . . the surprises you and mommy give us happen just like *(Snaps his finger)* that!

FATHER: Well, son . . . in God's timetable, it did happen just like *(Snap)* that. Remember how God tells us that a day is as a thousand years and a thousand years is as a day? In God's sight, that is.

BRAD: Well . . . I guess if God wanted to take a thousand years for a surprise, it's okay with me.

FATHER: I'm sure He appreciates your confidence, son. You see . . . it all came about, the surprise I mean, when the Jews expected an all-*conquering* Messiah, one who would help them throw off the slavery of Rome. The prophecies *did* speak of just such a leader. But . . . the prophecies also described a humble, suffering Messiah. The religious leaders of that day didn't really recognize that there were to be two advents.

BRAD: *Advent?* What's an advent?

FATHER: Advent? It means a coming . . . or a happening. We use it to describe the two comings of Jesus.

MARLA: You remember, Brad. The first advent was when Jesus was born. During this advent He went to the cross. The second advent is when He will come again to take us all to heaven and to set up the Mes . . . Mess. . . .

FATHER: Messianic.

MARLA: Messianic Kingdom.

FATHER: Well, Marla . . . you've remembered a great deal. The Jews didn't realize that Jesus came first to humble Himself and to go to the cross to redeem the world . . . *then* He was to return at a later time to establish the great Messianic Kingdom. That's the surprise ending I spoke of. They were surprised when He came, not as a conquering warrior . . . just a bit like television, Brad.

BRAD: That's a surprise a lot bigger than any television show! I don't understand it all, daddy, but if you say it's true . . . I believe you!

FATHER: It's true because it's what the Bible says, son. And it all came about just as the Bible said it would.

BRAD: Start from the beginning and tell it just the way it all happened.

MARLA: Begin way back when the prophets first told about it.

FATHER: All right! *(He settles back)* It all began way back when Isaiah, obeying God, spoke to Israel. . . .

(The lights fade from the jury stage. Isaiah steps through the center of curtain on the proscenium stage, onto the apron. As he does so, on the cue, "when Isaiah, obeying God, spoke to Israel" a soft spot picks him up and he is highlighted for the reading of the scroll which he holds in his hands. His entrance is timed so that as Mr. Carlson speaks the above cue lines, he (Isaiah) comes in immediately with his first line, "Thus saith the Lord," coming on the word "Israel."

ISAIAH: Thus saith the Lord! Behold, a virgin shall conceive and bear a son, and shall call his name Emmanuel, and the government shall be upon his shoulder; and his name shall be called . . . Wonderful . . . Counsellor . . . The Mighty God . . . The Everlasting Father . . . The Prince of Peace! Therefore, O Prophets, comfort my people, saith your God! Speak comfortably to Jerusalem; and cry unto her that her warfare is accomplished, that her iniquity is pardoned!

Shout the good tidings to Zion! Shout it from the mountains! Be not afraid! Say unto the cities of Judah, Behold your God! Arise! Shine! For your light is come! The Glory of the Lord is risen upon you! And the Glory of the Lord shall be revealed, and all flesh shall see it together; For the mouth of the Lord has spoken it!

(The spot fades from Isaiah and at its blackout, he steps back through the curtains. The curtains immediately part on a scene in the home of Mary. She is discovered at stage right, seated on a large pillow with her lap filled with sewing. To her left sits Ruth, also on a large pillow and sewing a garment. Between them is a low table on which is an assortment of sewing supplies and material. The room is that of a first century home in Galilee. As the curtains part, Ruth is speaking. They are both young women, probably in their late teens.

Ruth is outspoken and vivacious. Mary is quiet and calm in character.

RUTH: When you and Joseph are married. . . .

MARY: How many times must I tell you, Ruth, that I am only promised? It will be months before any announcement will be made and then many more months before the date is set for the marriage.

114

RUTH: You make it sound so far off.

MARY: These things do take time. I will admit, though, Joseph and I have discussed some plans for after we're married.

RUTH: My father says there is much work for carpenters in Jerusalem. Will you and Joseph be moving there? So many of the woodworkers are going there. The wages are very good.

MARY: No . . . I don't think we'll go there. There's also much work right here in Galilee. We both want to make our home here, near our people. We had thought of going back to Bethlehem where we both grew up, but not many of our people live there anymore.

RUTH: Yes . . . I remember. They left and came here after Herod destroyed their flocks.

MARY: Now Ruth . . . you know that isn't true. King Herod was merely carrying out orders from Rome. He had no choice.

RUTH: Oh . . . you always find *excuses* for people like Herod! He's a *bad* king! I think he actually enjoyed carrying out those orders.

MARY: You really shouldn't say such things, Ruth. You never know who may overhear you. Such rumors are usually just gossip, anyway.

RUTH: Oh, Mary, don't be so naive. Everyone knows that Herod is a puppet of Rome! Someday he'll get what he deserves!

MARY: Vengeance is Mine, saith the Lord.

RUTH: Well . . . what you say may be true, but why must we have to wait so long to be freed of such kings and . . . Rome?

MARY: Joseph was telling me just the other evening that the prophecy is soon to be fulfilled that Messiah will come. Oh, if only I could live to see that prophecy come true!

RUTH: Prophecy . . . prophecy . . . prophecy! ! Everyone's been talking about a Messiah for years and years . . . and *nothing* happens!

MARY: God has promised and I believe He will come . . . and soon!

RUTH: You act as if you were expecting Him to come walking through that door any moment.

MARY: *(Laughing softly)* Oh, Ruth . . . you're always so blunt. But, that's probably the reason you're so dear to me.

RUTH: Blunt? I'm just being realistic.

MARY: Blunt or realistic . . . I still enjoy your company. Don't ever stop coming to see me . . . I'd die of boredom.

RUTH: Which reminds me . . . I'd better get home and start the evening meal for my husband. There's real boredom . . . meal after meal after meal after meal! *(She begins folding her work and prepares to go.)*

MARY: *(Again laughing)* You aren't fooling me, Ruth. You adore cooking for that husband of yours and you know it!

RUTH: You're right, Mary. If it weren't for all my housework, I'd probably be bored to tears. I'll drop in tomorrow again. *(She rises and moves toward the door.)*

MARY: Do come, Ruth. I'd miss you if you didn't.

RUTH: *(Coming back and kissing Mary on the cheek)* I'd miss you too. *(Again she starts to go, then turns and says archly)* Let me know if Messiah should happen to march through your door!

MARY: *(Laughing gaily)* Ruth . . . you're impossible! *(Suddenly)* Oh . . . if you see Leah outside, ask her if she would get some fresh water from the well for the evening meal?

RUTH: All right, Mary, I will. Bye!

MARY: Thank you, Ruth. Good night.

(Ruth leaves. Mary looks after her for a moment. She smiles and gently shakes her head, giving the impression that she loves Ruth and is bemused by her attitudes. As she resumes her sewing, a soft voice is heard.)

GABRIEL: *(Softly)* Mary!

MARY: *(Not looking up from her work)* Is that you, Leah? *(There is no answer and Mary looks toward the door. Seeing no one, she resumes her sewing.)*

GABRIEL: *(Louder)* Mary!

(Mary looks up again and suddenly there is a blinding shaft of light from above, flooding her.)

MARY: *(Cringing away from this strange light, she gasps)* Who are you?

GABRIEL: Greetings, favored one of God! The Lord is with you!

MARY: *(She draws back)* Who are you? What do you want?

GABRIEL: Don't be afraid, Mary, for God has been gracious to you. I have been sent to tell you that this day you shall conceive and bear a Son and you shall call Him Jesus. He will be great; He will be called, The Son of the Most High; The Lord God will give Him the throne of David, and He will be King over Israel forever; His reign shall never end!

MARY: How can this be, since I have no husband?

GABRIEL: The Holy Spirit will come upon you, and the power of the Most High will overshadow you; and for that reason the Holy Child to be born will be called "The Son of God."

MARY: *(Questioningly)* The Son . . . of . . . God? . . . But . . . I.

GABRIEL: Why do you marvel at this? Your cousin Elisabeth has herself conceived in her old age; and she, though she was considered barren, is in her sixth month. But God's promises can never fail! With God nothing is impossible!

MARY: *(Kneeling before the angel)* I believe you! I bow to the will of God and will be obedient to what you have said.

(Mary bows her head, and as she remains motionless, the light slowly fades. Raising her head, holding herself erect on both

116

knees, extending her arms straight down to her sides, palms open flat to the front, looking straight overhead, a look of ecstasy on her face, she utters one short sentence.)

I am the handmaid of the Lord!

(She remains motionless, looking up directly overhead as the light slowly dims and she is once again alone. The curtain slowly closes.)

(Lights come up on jury stage when the proscenium curtains have closed. Mr. Carlson begins to speak as if just continuing the story.)

FATHER: . . . so you see, God's timetable was at last going to be fulfilled with the arrival of the Messiah.

BRAD: *(Looking up in the air as if in thought)* Daddy? *(Then looking at Mr. Carlson)* Was that a man angel, or a girl angel?

MARLA: *(Impatiently)* Oh, Brad . . . angels are always girls! Don't you remember the pictures in our Sunday school books?

BRAD: Then, how come one of them is called Gabriel? Gabriel's a boy's name!

FATHER: Brad's right, Marla. This angel who visited *Mary* was Gabriel. To tell the truth, all angels are referred to as being masculine.

MARLA: *(Triumphantly)* Then, how come in all the pageants at our church, women are always angels?

FATHER: Ah . . . well, you see . . . ah . . . *(Suddenly)* We're right in middle of our story. Is it all right if we discuss this matter a bit later?

MARLA: Well . . . all right . . . but don't forget!

FATHER: *(Wiping brow)* I'm sure I won't forget . . . I promise. *(Pause)* Now . . . where were we?

BRAD: *(Archly)* We just got rid of the angels!

FATHER: Oh . . . yes! Well . . . so . . . as Mary pondered over the thought that she was going to be the mother of Messiah, she began to . . . .

BRAD: *(Interrupting)* I thought His name was going to be Emmanuel?

FATHER: That's right.

BRAD: But . . . Gabriel just said he was to be called, Jesus. How come the *prophets* said His name would be Emmanuel, and Gabriel said Mary would call Him Jesus?

FATHER: *(Patiently)* How many names do you have, Brad?

BRAD: *(Counting on his fingers)* Brad . . . Bradley . . . Sherman . . . Carlson . . . Four!

FATHER: Oh, no . . . you've got more. Remember, your Uncle Fred calls you Shorty . . . and Grandfather calls you Sprout. Your

117

friends call you Speedy . . . Swifty . . . your mother calls you Darling . . . Button! Well . . . Jesus had many names too

MARLA: Sure . . . He was called Christ . . . Savior . . . Master . . . Lord . . .

BRAD: And Wonderful . . . Counselor . . . The Mighty God! I get it, daddy . . . Gabriel and the prophets just called Him by *one* of His names and that's why they were different. That's simple!

FATHER: Yup!

BRAD: *(Chin in his hand)* I wish an angel had named me!

FATHER: But, one did . . . your mother.

BRAD: I thought you said that . . . *(Father, Marla & Brad together)* all angels were masculine!

(All three burst into laughter.)

FATHER: I think we'd better get back to our story. *(Pause)* Even as Mary was visited by Gabriel, things were happening in God's timetable that would cause everything to come about just as the prophets had said they would. Remember, now . . . Mary and Joseph lived way up in Nazareth and had no intention of moving, or even visiting Bethlehem. Still . . . the prophets said Jesus was to be born there.

BRAD: Aw . . . I'm not worried! God will find a way!

FATHER: And He did Brad! This is how it happened!

(Jury stage lights begin to fade)

On day when King Herod and his ministers were holding court . . .

(Proscenium curtains open on the throne room in King Herod's palace. King Herod is upstage, center, sitting on a throne. To his left are two ministers. To his right, on either side of a doorway leading offstage, are two soldiers.
Sitting on the steps in front of and to the side of the throne are a number of women, paying close attention to what Herod is saying. Herod is speaking roughly and demandingly to a slave who is kneeling before him. A guard stands beside the slave with the butt of his spear holding the kneeling form almost prostrate before Herod. Herod, almost shouting, speaks.)

HEROD: And can you give me any reason why I should show you any leniency?

SLAVE: *(Pleading)* I was hungry, sire!

HEROD: Hungry? Well . . . if everyone that hungered stole from my storehouses, I'd end up a pauper! A pauper . . . do you hear? *(Gesturing in a casual way, but speaking with venom in his voice)* Take this miserable creature from my sight and have him flogged . . . then off to the galleys with him! Perhaps a few years of

118

pulling an oar will teach him that hunger is a poor excuse for thievery!

SLAVE: *(As he is being dragged away by the guard)* Mercy, sire! Mercy!

HEROD: *(Laughing without humor)* Mercy he wants! He should have thought better before he stole from the king! *(Suddenly)* Now, where is that messenger from Rome? I was told he was just arriving. Haven't I waited long enough? Bring him at once!

GUARD: *(Saluting, with clenched fist across his chest)* Yes, sire! At once!

HEROD: *(Angrily)* I'm surrounded by imbeciles! Imbeciles! *(The guard re-enters and salutes)* Well . . . where is he? Where's the messenger?

GUARD: He was detained at the gate, sire. He'll be here directly. They are identifying him.

HEROD: So! . . . I'm kept waiting while some corporal of the guard plays soldier? Don't they know a Roman courier when they see one?

1ST MIN: *(Leaning forward)* If sire will permit me. . . . It was your order that all who entered the palace gates must be searched and identified.

HEROD: How dare you suggest that I . . . . *(Coughs and stutters)* . . . I did? Well . . . .

2ND GUARD: *(Entering and saluting)* A Roman courier awaits an audience, sire!

HEROD: Yes, yes, yes . . . show him in . . . show him in!

COURIER: *(Shown in, he salutes)* Hail, oh mighty Herod.

HEROD: Hail, Roman! Welcome to Jerusalem. What brings you?

COURIER: A dispatch from Rome, sire. Caesar Augustus also sends you his warmest greetings and trusts that the gods have honored you.

HEROD: *(Accepting dispatch)* Caesar's words do me honor. May I offer you the hospitality of my palace? What is your pleasure?

COURIER: I ask only for food, drink and a fresh mount so that I may be on my way. My orders are to make all haste to complete my mission. You are most gracious to offer me other hospitalities, but I must decline and only hope that some day I may return and accept your invitation.

HEROD: One moment, then, and I will see if Caesar wishes an answer, and you may have anything you wish and be on your way, if that is your desire.

(Herod reads the dispatch with much grunting and muttering. From time to time he looks up and then resumes reading. Finally he finishes . . . . rolls up the dispatch. Hands it back to him.)

I can't say that this comes as a complete surprise. I see that these

119

orders cover all of Rome's colonies . . . . and they are striking orders! In fact, they cover the whole world! I also see that you have only Egypt left to visit and then home to Rome. Don't you think a night's rest here at the palace would give you much needed relaxation and better fit you for your journey?

COURIER: There is added incentive, sire, to the completion of my journey. I wish to return to Rome in time for the games. If the gods favor me, I may win my promotion, sire.

HEROD: A most worthy endeavor, Roman! Guard . . . see that the courier is refreshed, give him one of my finest horses and see him safely on his way to the coast. *(To courier)* Return to Caesar and give him my most earnest greetings. Tell him I shall carry out his wishes at once! A safe journey to you.

COURIER: Thank you, sire. May the gods protect you. *(Salutes)* Hail Caesar! *(Courier turns to go)*

HEROD: Oh, Courier. *(Courier stops and turns back to him)* Good luck in the games at Rome. What is your name, so that I may follow your fortune in the news from Rome?

COURIER: Petronius, sire . . . and thank you for your good wishes. It is my great desire to be appointed a Centurion.

HEROD: Should you win your appointment, come to Jerusalem and serve with *me* in Caesar's Empire. Farewell, Roman!

COURIER: Hail, Caesar! *(Courier leaves)*

HEROD: *(Turning to his ministers)* Gentlemen . . . the orders from Caesar are very brief and to the point . . . everyone in the province is to be taxed. It is his decree that this should start at once! It is simple enough, so I leave it in your hands. Since all must be taxed, proceed the same as we do in levying taxes in the cities. Just apply it to cover the entire province. I shall sign the decree after you have drawn it up for me.

1st MIN: This poses a problem, sire.

HEROD: Problem? Since when is taxation a problem?

1st MIN: This conquered people do not stay in any one place. They are nomadic, and move about throughout the land.

2nd MIN: It would take an army to hunt them out, sire — judge their ability to pay and collect it. Being a wandering people, they could easily misrepresent their wealth and possessions and avoid rightful taxes.

HEROD: I see what you mean. What would you suggest?

1st MIN: Perhaps the answer is to tax them all equally . . . for every person a fixed tax.

HEROD: No . . . that's not the answer. It's been tried before. Some couldn't pay and we would have to throw them into prison. This would cause a great deal of unrest, as it always does, and we would have to have another army to keep peace. No, that isn't the answer. I have enough troubles without risking an open rebellion.

1st Min: If there were only a way to make them gather together in an orderly way . . . quickly and without force.

Herod: *(Sarcastically)* Yes . . . have them parade past me and drop their taxes in my hand, because they *love* me so much! If you can't think of a sensible way, minister, I'd suggest that you . . . *(Suddenly)* Wait! Maybe you have something there! *(Slowly)* We'll make these *nomads,* as you call them, do our work for us! Get charcoal and board and take this down.

(2nd Min. leaves to get the required charcoal and board. Herod speaks approvingly to 1st Min.)

Sometimes you do show a bit of ingenuity.

1st Min: Thank you, sire . . . I am here to serve.

(2nd Min. leaves to get the required charcoal and board. Herod

Herod: Now let's see . . . yes! Write this down! It is my decree, effective at once . . . . that all subjects of this Province shall muster in the city of his people or place of his descent, that an estimate may be taken of their persons and possessions! . . . . This to be done, that a fair and equitable tax may be gathered. *(Spoken to ministers)* Wouldn't you say that that ought to do the job pretty well? *(The ministers nod and Herod continues)* This order given under my hand and seal this day and to be carried out under pain of death! . . . Now, see to it that every city and village has this decree read and posted before its inhabitants.

1st Min: One moment, sire! Shouldn't there be a time limit set to this decree?

Herod: Time limit? Oh . . . yes! A time limit . . . now . . . let's see! Caesar would be pleased if we accomplished it immediately . . . perhaps by . . . . I have it! *(To scribe)* Add this to the decree: All mustering of the people must be accomplished and completed by the feast day of the god Janus. So be it!

2nd Min: By having it completed before January 1st, all our legions will be back in Jerusalem for our games and that will insure a goodly crowd and much wagering.

1st Min: Not to mention the best of gladiators available to compete. You have perfected a stroke of genius, sire!

Herod: *(Wearily)* Yes, yes, yes, yes . . . but all these matters of state have whetted my appetite. Bring me a basket of fruit and send for the Royal Magician to entertain us; I am weary of "looking out" for all my loyal subjects . . . . *(Clapping)* Well . . . . where is the fruit and the Royal Magician? Must I wait until I'm bored? Sometimes I wish I had been born with the simple tastes of a shepherd rather than a king!

(Curtain on proscenium. Lights up on jury stage.)

121

FATHER: In the very near future the whole world would be taxed.

BRAD: He was a crafty old king, wasn't he?

MARLA: Daddy . . . did that mean that *all* the people had to travel to another place?

FATHER: All those who had moved away from their birthplace or where their families lived.

MARLA: That means Joseph and Mary had to go back to Bethlehem, then?

FATHER: Right! Remember . . . Mary told Ruth that that was where both she and Joseph were born . . . so . . . it meant they had to travel also.

MARLA: Were Joseph and Mary married by then?

FATHER: Oh, yes! Joseph was working as a carpenter up in Nazareth.

BRAD: Sure, Marla . . . . don't you remember how the angel came to Joseph and said, "Don't be afraid to get married to Mary, Joseph, because everything that's happening is God's way of getting things done!" Right, daddy?

FATHER: A rather free translation, but I'll buy it!

MARLA: Then . . . then . . . God planned it all this way so Mary would have to go to Bethlehem?

FATHER: *(Laughing)* Well-l . . . theologians would argue a bit with that simple philosophy, but essentially that is what happened.

BRAD: That means the prophecy *would* come true if Jesus were born while they were in Bethlehem!

FATHER: You have the picture exactly. Mary and Joseph way up in Nazareth had to travel far to the south to Bethlehem to be certain they paid the proper tax . . . . the result being, Jesus could be born exactly where the prophets foretold.

MARLA: *(Thoughtfully)* Boy . . . all that way . . . just to pay taxes! They sure make it awfully easy for *you* to pay *your* taxes, don't they, daddy?

FATHER: Now, that's a new one. How do you come up with that opinion?

MARLA: Why . . . you just write it down on a piece of paper . . . put it in an envelope . . . mail it . . . quick . . . easy . . . simple!

FATHER: *(Chuckling)* Well . . . I guess if you look at it in that way, it is a fairly simple operation. I'll have to explain that to my accountant. It will be new to him, I'm sure! Maybe I can convince him to lower his fee!

BRAD: What happened next, daddy?

FATHER: Well . . . events moved swiftly. Mary's baby was due most any time, but in spite of this, she and Joseph had to journey to Bethlehem. They had made all the preparations, but Joseph was worried and quite concerned over Mary making the difficult trip.

(Jury lights fade and proscenium curtain opens.)

122

(Scene: Interior of Joseph and Mary's home. Mary is sewing and Joseph works at completing a cradle. Mary sits stage left; Joseph works stage right)

MARY: *(Stopping her sewing for a moment)* That's such a beautiful cradle, Joseph.

JOSEPH: *(Busy working on a leg of the cradle)* I only wish we could take it to Bethlehem with us so that when our child is born we could make use of it right away.

MARY: You seem so sure that our baby will be born in Bethlehem.

JOSEPH: *(Stops working)* The prophecies tell us that the "Redeemer of Israel" will be born there. Didn't the angel tell us that our son is to be Israel's chosen leader? So . . . We're going to Bethlehem . . . your time is very near, and the angel said . . . .

MARY: *(Laughing)* Wait . . . stop! I surrender! Oh, Joseph, my love . . . . you are so *intense* when you talk about our child.

JOSEPH: It is because of the great responsibility we have, Mary! Just think! Our *Son* will be the great leader of Israel! My mind and heart can scarcely comprehend all that God has . . . "wrapped up" . . . in that precious life you are carrying in you!

MARY: Yes, I know, my husband . . . I also find my heart filled with the wonder of it all. Sometimes it is as if I cannot bear to think about it . . . the great truth we have had entrusted to our keeping.

JOSEPH: *(Rising and going over to her)* And I worry about you, Mary. Your time is so close at hand and I fear that the long journey will cause you great harm!

MARY: *(She looks up, reaches up and takes one of Joseph's hands in hers)* Joseph . . . . God will lead us! "Though I walk through the valley of the shadow of death, I will fear no evil!" I'm not afraid.

JOSEPH: *(Kneeling beside her, still holding her hand)* I shall never know why God has blessed me with such a woman as you. Surely, my cup overflows!

MARY: *(Looking at his hands — turning them over as he talks)* I'm sure that God knew when he brought me you, that your strong hands, gentleness, and trusting faith would make you a fitting father for our son!

JOSEPH: Mary! That's the first time I have heard you refer to our child as our . . . *Son!*

MARY: My husband forgets that the angel Gabriel spoke to me and said . . . . *(She suddenly stops and looks at Joseph)* Oh! . . . you're teasing me!

JOSEPH: *(Laughing gently, teasingly)* You know . . . *(Lightly touching her nose)* . . . the tip of your nose wiggles when you talk . . . and when you blush . . . like right now . . . it starts at the tip of your ears and runs way . . . .

MARY: *(Playfully slapping his hand away)* Honestly, Joseph . . .

you're such a tease . . . *(Serio-comically)* I don't think I shall go
to Bethlehem after all!

JOSEPH: That means *I* can ride the donkey. *(Mary laughs)* Why are
you laughing?

MARY: Oh, Joseph! Can't you see yourself? Your long legs . . .
dragging and bumping! It would look much more equal if *you*
carried the donkey!

JOSEPH: *(After they both laugh)* Speaking of the trip . . . perhaps we
had better get our rest. Tomorrow will be our first day and you
must not be allowed to get too tired. I only wish I had something more than just a donkey for you to ride. But . . . we must
be thankful . . . . we wouldn't even have a donkey except that
Ruth's husband insisted we borrow one of his.

MARY: It will do nicely, Joseph. Why . . . when I was a little girl,
we used to ride donkeys just for fun. I'll simply pretend I'm a
little girl!

JOSEPH: *(Standing up and offering his hand)* Come, then . . . it grows
late . . . *(Pause) Little Girl!*

They exit laughing. Curtain closes. Lights come up on jury stage.

FATHER: "Now, when Jesus was born in Bethlehem of Judea in the
days of Herod the king, behold, there came wise men from the
east to Jerusalem. . . ."

BRAD: Who were these kings, daddy?

FATHER: No one really knows, Brad. There is very little known about
them . . . who they were . . . where they came from. We only
know what few words are spoken of them in the Scriptures. Tradition has given them names, but all we really know of them is
that the Bible tells us they had followed a star, visited Herod,
worshiped the newborn child and were warned in a dream not to
return to Herod, but go home another way.

MARLA: Why do you suppose they went to Herod in the first place?

FATHER: Well . . . let us suppose that it happened in this way. After
following the star as far as Jerusalem . . .

(Fade jury stage lights)

. . . they entered the city . . .

*(Proscenium curtain opens, again revealing Herod's throne room.
The two ministers are again to his left — the guards at the door.
One guard has moved forward, saluted, and is speaking.)*

GUARD: Sire . . . a merchant is outside . . . requesting an audience.

HEROD: Why am I constantly saddled with these mewling merchants?
First they want protection . . . then they want freedom to charge
more . . . and then they make a big fuss when they have to pay
for these privileges! If it isn't one thing . . . it's another! Well . . .
what does he want?

GUARD: He will speak only to you, sire. He seems unusually disturbed.

HEROD: (*Resignedly*) All right . . . send him in. (*The guard leaves*)
So . . . he's disturbed! Well, if his coming and interrupting me
means nothing, he'll be pretty disturbed by the time he leaves.
I can't afford to ignore these puppets, but I don't have to be nice
if his coming is just some petty grievance that one of my ministers could have easily settled.

GUARD: (*Returning with merchant*) Merchant Philius, sire.

MERCH: (*After bowing*) Hail, oh king! My coming is of great urgency!

HEROD: You merchants are always in a state of urgency! Well, what
is it this time? Which has been violated . . . your pride or your
pocketbook?

MERCH: Neither, sire. It is regarding three strangers within the city!

HEROD: (*A little angry*) Three strangers? Did you interrupt my day
to tell me that there are three strangers in Jerusalem. . . . There
are thousands of strangers entering Jerusalem every day!

MERCH: But these are mysterious travelers, sire. They appear to be
very wealthy and their caravan includes well over fifty camels,
well loaded, sire!

HEROD: So much the better for our trading. Is this all you had to
tell me?

MERCH: Oh, no, sire! The three strangers wear insignia that show
that they are either very highborn citizens or perhaps kings!

HEROD: (*Suddenly sitting upright*) Kings? (*Turning to ministers*)
Why haven't I been told of this?

1st MIN: This is the first we have heard of this, sire!

HEROD: Humph! Jerusalem could be overrun by brigands before you
would hear of it! Now I have to depend upon *merchants* to make
known what's happening in the city! (*Turning to merchant*) Tell
me all you know of these strangers.

MERCH: They arrived early today, sire! They have sent messengers
throughout the city asking a strange question.

HEROD: Question! What kind of question?

MERCH: Where is he that is born King of the Jews?

HEROD: (*Standing abruptly*) King of the Jews? There is no King but
Herod! Who dares challenge my throne?

MERCH: (*Cringing, but daring to speak again*) There is more, sire!

HEROD: More? Ah, yes! They must *know* of this . . . *king!* Does he
have a name . . . followers? Quickly, man . . . what more?

MERCH: They don't know where he is, sire! They only speak of a
star . . . His Star . . . they call it. All they say is that they have
come to worship him, sire!

HEROD: (*Furious*) Worship him? *Worship him!* How dare . . . !
(*Suddenly quiet*) (*Sitting again*) Wait! You say they know not
where he is?

MERCH: That is right, sire! They and their messengers have asked
nearly everyone in high places, except here at the palace. The

125

people in the city are in an uproar over it! Even now there is a mob gathering before the palace gates. They want to know who these strangers are! There are rumors that they are spies sent to search out the secrets of Jerusalem's defenses!

HEROD: *(Angrily and impatiently)* Bah! A tempest in a teapot! The rabble in the streets are always ready to imagine the worst! If they are spies . . . do you think they would announce their presence in this manner? For that matter, what enemy would even think of challenging the might of Rome? The rabble makes me sick with their lunatic reasoning! Rome has sent no word of any threats! *(Suddenly quiet)* But, what intrigues me is their search for a King of the Jews. *(He turns to his ministers)* Send word to the chief priests and scribes. Tell them to send their leaders to me at once! If there is a King of the Jews prophesied in their Scriptures, they will perhaps know where He is to be born, or at least some hint . . . *(Craftily)* they'll know . . . and then . . . *(With a gesture)* . . . send for them!

1st MIN: Yes, sire.

(As the two ministers turn to leave, the lights black out slowly. At the same time, Herod waves his arm, dismissing the merchant, who bows out the door.)

(The lights are blacked out only a few moments. During the blackout, the ministers return and a number of priests and scribes take their places before the throne. When the lights come back on, slowly, Herod is speaking.)

HEROD: . . . and I knew that if a King of the Jews were to come, of course you of the Temple would surely know His whereabouts. Where is He to be born?

PRIEST: A King, your majesty? A deliverer . . . yes, . . . but a King?

HEROD: *(Impatiently)* Call Him what you like, but is there such a prophecy?

PRIEST: *(Shrugging)* Oh . . . hundreds of years ago there was some such belief.

HEROD: *(Relaxing)* Hundreds of years ago?

PRIEST: Yes . . . when our people were in captivity in Babylon. Our Scriptures, written at that time, spoke of a Messiah . . . a deliverer.

HEROD: And if He came today . . . . He would deliver you from the Romans? Would you expect Him to displace me, too?

PRIEST: *(Chuckling)* Your Majesty! Your Majesty! If we believed everything written hundreds of years ago, we'd be so busy chasing fantasies, we'd have no time for our Temple duties!

HEROD: *(Searchingly)* I have a feeling you're evading my question!

PRIEST: All right, sire . . . there is a prophecy. I guessed your reason for bringing us here and I came prepared. I shall read what our ancient prophets wrote. But I warn you, sire . . . it gives no date or time.

126

(He reaches for a scroll, held by another priest, unrolls it and reads.)

"And Thou Bethlehem, in the land of Judah, art not the least among the Princes of Judah, for out of thee shall come a Governor, that shall rule my people Israel."

(The priest rolls up the scroll as he speaks.)

So . . . you see, your Majesty, this so-called *king,* if there is such a person, has been prophesied as coming from Bethlehem. We of the Temple do not believe in such tales . . . especially such ancient ones!

HEROD: *(Thinking before he speaks)* You are very cynical. Don't you Temple leaders even believe the ancient prophecies of your religion?

PRIEST: We believe only in today, sire.

HEROD: Well . . . I have a little surprise for you. I have invited the three strangers who have come to Jerusalem seeking this Messiah of yours. Evidently they believe in your ancient prophecies more than you do. You will remain while I interrogate them. *(Turning to his minister)*

(The minister gestures to the guard at the door. He leaves immediately.)

HEROD: It will be interesting to see what they have to say when I mention that Bethlehem is their destination.

PRIEST: *(Sarcastically)* Only fools accept a fool's errand! I assure you, nothing can come of such a fool's quest!

HEROD: And I assure you, I shall take measures to make sure!

GUARD: *(Coming in and saluting Herod)* Sire . . . the three strangers await your pleasure.

HEROD: Show them in, guard.

(The guard goes to the door, stands to the upstage side, and strikes the floor three times with the butt end of his spear.)

GUARD: Send in the three strangers!

(Enter the three wise men. The priests, meanwhile have taken their places to the left of the throne and downstage. The three strangers come to the right and slightly downstage of the throne. They kneel before Herod. Herod nods his head to them.)

HEROD: Welcome to my palace. Please . . . please rise. I perceive that you have come a long way and you must be weary. My palace is at your disposal. I also see that you are not ordinary travelers. Who are you and what is your mission that brings you into Judea?

(The three men rise. One steps forward)

MELCH: It is true, your Majesty, we have come a long way. In our native lands we are known as wise men. *(He indicates Casper)* This is Casper, ancient seer of the Apothecrin. *(Casper bows deeply and as he straightens up, he claps his hands. A bearer comes in quickly with a large box and sets it before Herod. He quickly leaves.)*

CASPER: Your Majesty . . . a most humble gift of rare perfumes which I hope pleases you.

HEROD: *(Nodding and making a slight gesture)* Your gift is most honored.

MELCH: *(Indicating Balthazar)* This is Balthazar, ancient seer of Anthorizon. *(Balthazar also bows deeply and as he straightens up, claps his hands. A bearer enters with a large box and also sets it before Herod and quickly leaves.)*

BALTH: Your Majesty . . . may I add my humble gift? The finest silks from the Orient.

HEROD: *(Again nodding and making a slight gesture)* I am honored.

MELCH: And I am Melchior . . . ancient seer of the Orinian. *(He bows and as he straightens up, also claps. A bearer enters with another box, though much smaller.)* Precious jewels from the lands far to the south of Ethiopia.

HEROD: *(Nods his head and again gestures)* You do me great honor.

MELCH: My companions and I have a simple request, sire. We have followed a star that has led us this far. Strangely, it has disappeared. We come, seeking a child.

HEROD: A child? What manner of child?

MELCH: The ancient prophecies say that He is King of the Jews and we have come to pay Him homage.

HEROD: A child who is called the King of the Jews . . . and you say you have followed a star? And now that star has disappeared?

MELCH: Yes. It led us here and so we feel that whatever power has brought us this far expects us to find the answer here in the logical place, the center of Judaism.

HEROD: You have reasoned well, Melchior. *(Indicates the priests and scribes)* These leaders of the Temple are at your service.

PRIEST: *(Stepping forward)* We have searched the ancient scrolls and have found that whatever you seek will be found in Bethlehem of Judea.

MELCH: Bethlehem! *(Turning to his companions)* Our long journey will soon be over. *(He turns back to the priest)* Thank you for the knowledge you have given to us. *(To Herod)* By your leave, sire . . . we would continue our journey. You have been most kind.

HEROD: I would be remiss in my kingly obligations if I were not to lend you all possible assistance. Tell me . . . what do you expect to find in Bethlehem?

MELCH: We do not know, your Majesty. We have been led by a

strange and wonderful urging to do what we are doing. When we find the child, no matter when, or where, we will but pay Him homage. *(Turning to the priests)* We find it strange that you, the leaders of Judaism, do not seek out this King!

PRIEST: *(Haughtily)* Perhaps we find *one* king sufficient!

HEROD: *(Quickly)* Go and search for this King. When you have found Him, bring me word of His whereabouts *(Humbly, but with hidden meaning in his words)* that I may come and worship him also!

MELCH: *(Bowing)* By your leave, then, your Majesty.
(The three Wise Men bow deeply and leave.)

HEROD: *(Thoughtfully)* One thing for sure . . . . *(Looks meaningfully at the priest)* . . . They are not fools!

PRIEST: *(Bowing low)* By your leave, your Majesty.
(All the priests and scribes bow low and exit.)

HEROD: *(Looking after them)* I think it would be wise to keep a sharp eye on them . . . *(He indicates the departed priests with a finger)* I don't think they'd be foolish enough to claim a new king . . . but . . . I shall never be accused of turning my back on such. *(Then, to his ministers)* Alert my personal guard that as soon as these Wise Men return and tell us where this *king* is, we shall pay Him the *homage* He deserves!

(Curtain closes on a thoughtful Herod. Jury stage lights come up.)

BRAD: I don't believe Herod really wanted to pay homage to Jesus!

FATHER: No . . . he was only concerned that another king would come and take away his throne! As the Bible tells us . . . he only wanted the Wise Men to reveal the whereabouts of Jesus so that he could destroy Him before He became a threat to his power.

BRAD: I remember what happened! An angel told the Wise Men, in a dream, what Herod was up to and told them to return home by a road that didn't go through Jerusalem, so Herod wouldn't learn from them just where Jesus was.

MARLA: That must have made Herod very angry!

FATHER: So angry, he sent out a decree that all Jewish boy babies, two years and under, should be killed, hoping that the baby king would be among those slain.

MARLA: What a terrible thing to do!

BRAD: Daddy . . . aren't we forgetting about Mary and Joseph? What's happening to them?

FATHER: Well . . . it was a trying time for both of them. Mary was very close to the time when her baby would be born . . . and Joseph was sick with worry over the hardship of riding all the way from Nazareth to Bethlehem on a donkey.

MARLA: I can't imagine riding all that way on a donkey! But . . . I guess they didn't have cars and trains and ambulances in those days.

BRAD: I think it would be fun riding a donkey all that way!

MARLA: Aren't you forgetting how stiff you were last summer when you rode the pony all afternoon up at Uncle Jim's farm?

BRAD: That's right! Did Mary have to ride all afternoon?

FATHER: I'm afraid much longer than that! From Nazareth to Bethlehem was a few days' journey in those days. The roads were very poor . . . probably little better than trails, and there were mountainous hills with much twisting and turning. A donkey doesn't walk very fast, so it was likely a rough, weary trip under difficult conditions.

BRAD: I hadn't thought of it as that long and hard. I've changed my mind . . . I'll go by airplane!

FATHER: (Laughing) That's as good a solution as I could have wished!

MARLA: Did they stay with friends when they arrived?

FATHER: Marla! You know that answer to that!

MARLA: I know, daddy . . . but I like the way you tell it . . . I'm only teasing!

FATHER: Well . . . when they arrived, tired, hungry and dusty . . . there was quite a shock awaiting them! Hundreds of other travelers, having to come to Bethlehem, the same as they, were ahead of them! Remember last summer when we were traveling out west and couldn't find a motel with any vacancies that one night?

BRAD: Boy . . . I'll say! We had to sleep in the car!

MARLA: I thought it was fun!

BRAD: Well . . . I didn't!

FATHER: Well . . . about the same thing happened to Joseph and Mary. It was probably late at night. They knocked at the door of the inn and . . .

(Jury lights fade and curtain opens on roadway just outside an inn. It is night and Joseph is walking up to the door of the inn. He walks with his arm around Mary who is at his side. They stop at the door and Joseph, lovingly and reassuringly, pats Mary's hand, then turns to knock. The door is suddenly thrown open.)

INNK: (Innkeeper leans out and yells roughly) If you're looking for rooms, there are none!

JOSEPH: (Patiently) We've come a long way, sir, and we are very tired. There is no other inn and the night is. . . .

INNK: (Quickly interrupting) I tell you there is no room here. Every room and corner is taken!

(He starts to close the door, but Joseph puts out his hand.)

JOSEPH: (Insistently) But, you don't understand! My wife is near her time and I fear for her safety during the cold night! Please . . .

130

you must have at least space enough for her . . . I'll sleep outside . . . only take her in!

INNK: *(Hands outstretched in hopeless gesture)* Now, look! I appreciate your concern . . . I'm also concerned! But for the last time . . . I just don't have an inch of space left!

JOSEPH: Perhaps a place just by the fire?

INNK: *(Shrugging)* What can I say that will convince you? It seems that every Jew in the Province has knocked on this door and all are as desperate as you. For the last time . . . I can't do anything for you!

JOSEPH: But . . . !

INNK: No! Now, be off or I'll. . . .

(The Innkeeper's wife appears at the door.) She is businesslike and rather blunt.)

WIFE: What is it, Benjamin? *(She sees Joseph and Mary)* Oh . . . more travelers! Well . . . we've no room, so close the door. There's no use heating the outdoors! *(She turns to go and then looks at Mary more closely. Suddenly she speaks gently.)* Why . . . Benjamin . . . she's little more than a girl! *(To Mary)* How tired you must be!

JOSEPH: *(Putting his arm about Mary)* Very tired! All we are asking is shelter for the night, even if it's on the bare floor. The time for her child is very near and I fear for my wife's safety in the chill of the night air!

WIFE: *(To her husband)* Are you certain there's nothing?

INNK: You *know* there isn't!

WIFE: *(Helplessly)* We . . . we just can't turn them away! She may lose her child. Remember how we lost our only child on a night like this, Benjamin. There must be some place . . . .

INNK: *(Quickly)* I tell you, woman . . . there is nothing!

WIFE: *(Suddenly remembering)* Wait! *(Pointing offstage right)* Around to the rear, under the inn, is a large stable. I'm sure there must be at least one empty stall there! It isn't much, but it will be a roof and shelter from the cold. The hay is plentiful and it will make a soft bed for you. *(To husband)* Is it all right, Benjamin?

INNK: Well . . . certainly, if they don't mind sleeping in a barn!

JOSEPH: May God bless you!

WIFE: *(Pointing)* Just go around to the back and you'll see the gate into the barnyard. Be sure to close it after you so the sheep don't wander out. *(To Mary)* We lost our baby many years ago, but I've kept the swaddling clothes in hope that perhaps some day . . . you may have them just in case the child should come tonight.

MARY: You are very kind!

JOSEPH: Come, Mary . . . we must get you in out of the night air. *(Curtain closes as they move offstage. Jury lights come up. Mr. Carlson is speaking.)*

FATHER: And that's the way it happened. Mary had her baby that very night. In the overcrowded inn there was eating and drinking and merrymaking. There, it was warm and bright. Just a short distance away a baby was born in a stable . . . the Son of God! In the inn they said, "There is no room for you . . . we have no place here for you to rest your head!" They said this to Him who was destined to say, "Come unto me all ye who are weary and are heavy laden and I will give you rest!"

BRAD: Do you suppose those people in the inn ever found out that a King was born under the inn?

FATHER: The Bible doesn't say whether or not the people in the inn ever paid any attention to what was happening in the stable, but they probably never even knew what took place that night.

BRAD: Well, maybe they read it in the newspaper or heard it over the radio!

MARLA: Silly! They didn't have newspapers and radio way back there!

BRAD: Says who?

FATHER: That's right, Brad. It's true, there were no headlines in the papers because there were none in those days. There was no television or radio in those days either . . . but there *was* something more tremendous, more wonderful and much more exciting than any of these on that night!

BRAD: *(Excitedly)* You mean when the three Wise Men came to see Jesus, daddy?

MARLA: No, silly . . . that wasn't very big! It must be something bigger than that!

BRAD: Bigger? What could be bigger than that? Can you name any other baby who was ever born where *three kings* came to the hospital to see him when he was born . . . and even better than that . . . came to a barn?

FATHER: That's pretty good thinking . . . but that's not it.

BRAD: It isn't? What was it then?

FATHER: Well . . . here's what it says in the Bible. *(Picks up Bible)* "And there were shepherds in the same country abiding in the fields . . .

(Lights fade on jury stage and curtain opens on proscenium.)

. . . keeping watch over their flocks by night . . . .

(Curtain opens on a rocky glen. It is night and the shepherds are sitting, lying or standing in various positions about or near a fire that is center stage and down front. A young shepherd boy speaks to his father.)

BOY: Aren't the stars bright tonight, father?

FATHER: Yes, my son. It seems as if one might almost reach up and touch them!

BOY: And how still the night is.

FATHER: Now that you mention it, it *is* still! Never have I felt such quiet!

1ST SHEP: I for one am glad that it's still . . . the sheep are resting quietly. If a wind were blowing they might get restless and hard to manage.

FATHER: Son . . . why don't you play your instrument? Perhaps a quiet little song will help keep the sheep calm.

BOY: Yes, father.

(The boy plays a plaintive little melody. Perhaps a young boy who plays the flute can be chosen to play the part of the shepherd boy. If not, someone offstage can play and the boy can pantomime the playing.)

2ND SHEP: That was a good melody . . . give us another.

BOY: *(About to play)* Look, father . . . isn't *that* a bright star? I don't remember ever seeing that one before!

FATHER: *(Looking to where the boy points)* It *is* bright, isn't it? You're right . . . I've never seen it before, either! Wait! . . . it's moving! What a strange thing . . . No! . . . it's *not* moving, it's getting brighter, . . . and larger . . . . ! *(Light begins to grow and shepherds all move as some rise up, others cringe and shield their eyes. As light grows, a deep thunder begins to throb.)*

BOY: What is it, father?

FATHER: I don't know! *(Suddenly it is a blinding, shimmering brightness! The thunderous sound builds up to a climax . . . then suddenly ceases! The shepherds all fall back in terror as the boy's father exclaims.)* MERCIFUL GOD IN HEAVEN!

(Suddenly a voice fills the air.)

ANGEL: Do not be afraid, Shepherds! I bring you good news! This is a time for your people to *rejoice!* For I bring you word that today in the little town of Bethlehem a Savior is born who is the Christ! When you find Him, you will know it is He, for He will be wrapped in swaddling clothes and His cradle will be a manger.

(The shepherds, no longer afraid, gaze up in awe. A flood of angelic music surges up — The angelic voices can be taped. A choir can sing a series of "Glorias" or a live chorus can sing the words, "Glory to God in the Highest, etc. . . ." It swells to a crescendo and then gradually fades away and along with it the light. Finally there are no more voices and the lights are back to normal.)

1ST SHEP: What a tremendous sight! What does it mean?

FATHER: Did you hear what the angel said?

BOY: He said that Messiah has come!

2ND SHEP: But, what did it mean? Wrapped in swaddling clothes and His cradle a manger?

FATHER: Yes . . . I always thought Messiah would be born in kingly surroundings! But . . . to be born in a stall for cattle! Perhaps it was an hallucination!

1ST SHEP: No . . . it was real . . . we all saw and heard the same thing!

FATHER: Then we must go and find this child! Yes . . . we must go into Bethlehem and look into every stable, barn and cattle-shed! If the Angel of the Lord revealed it to us . . . then we are expected to find Him and proclaim it to everyone!

BOY: May I come too, father?

FATHER: Yes, my son . . . you may come. If this is truly the Messiah, you must see Him, for some day you will march in His all-conquering army that shall free us from the Roman yoke!

(To another shepherd)

Josiah, you and Nathan remain with the flock. We will go into Bethlehem and see this thing of which the angel spoke. *(To the others)* Come . . . we must hurry!

(All but two leave, as the curtain closes. Jury lights come up.)

MARLA: That must have been the most exciting night of that shepherd boy's life!

FATHER: And in the lives of all the shepherds! *(Looking at Brad)* Brad . . . you look as if you were a million miles away!

BRAD: I was just thinking . . . there was the flood . . . and the ten plagues of Egypt . . . Elijah going to heaven in a whirlwind . . . the crossing of the Red Sea . . . the falling of the walls of Jericho . . . the Ten Commandments and a few others . . . but . . . you're right, daddy . . . I guess that a whole sky filled with millions of angels is the *greatest!* Even greater than television, radio . . . or anything like that!

FATHER: Of course . . . this was tremendous, but we can't rule out an even greater event than all these. Can you guess what one I'm talking about?

MARLA: Well . . . I thought of just one more when Brad stopped . . . I think it must have been the Resurrection!

BRAD: *(Filled with awe)* That's right! I guess that would top them all!

FATHER: Right! But, that's a story for another night. As for tonight's story, everything worked out according to God's Plan! The prophecies were fulfilled . . . . *(Picking up Bible again)* . . . Jesus was born just as the prophets said He would be. And, as all good things must end, so ends our story for tonight.

BRAD: Wait a minute, daddy! You forgot two things . . . . How the shepherds found Jesus in the barn . . . and when the Wise Men came.

FATHER: Well . . . let's see! We can't very well leave the shepherds wandering about the Judean hills, can we?

MARLA: That's right! And we can't leave the Wise Men just . . . just.

FATHER: *(Helping her)* . . . star-gazing?

MARLA: That's it, daddy . . . star-gazing!

FATHER: I'm afraid there isn't much said in the Bible about their visit. Most Bible scholars even say that the Wise Men came at a different time to see Jesus, too, so we'll have to . . .

BRAD: *(Quickly interrupting)* But, daddy . . . all the manger scenes show both the Wise Men *and* the shepherds there at the same time!

FATHER: That's true, Brad. No one can be sure just when the Wise Men came. One thing is sure, though . . . the shepherds came the same night Jesus was born.

BRAD: Daddy . . . why not tell it just as if both the Wise Men and the shepherds came the same night? I'm sure God won't mind.

FATHER: All right . . . . I guess it won't do any harm. After all, how do we *know* that it didn't happen just that way? So . . . we'll make the manger scene *come to life!*

BRAD: That'll be *super*, daddy!

FATHER: So . . . it's all settled. *(Pause)* Let's see, now . . . where shall we start? Oh, yes! There they are, Mary and Joseph, all settled cozy and warm in the barn. That night Jesus was born and Mary wrapped Him in swaddling clothes and laid Him in the manger where He promptly fell asleep. Mary was soon fast asleep on the sweet-smelling hay nearby, and Joseph, much too excited to sleep, stood by a small window, keeping watch and thinking about all that had happened. As he gazed out into the moonlit night, he remembered that it had been a long time since the angel had appeared to him in a dream and bade him have no fear in marrying Mary. Now it was many months later and there had been no further sign from God that truly this newborn baby was the One the angel had claimed Him to be. And yet, even as he thought anxiously on these things, his unconscious and unspoken prayer was about to be answered in the events that quickly happened that same night. Through them Joseph and Mary knew without any doubt that their Son was truly the child of promise! *(Jury lights begin to dim.)* Suddenly there were voices outside the stable door.

The lights dim on the jury stage. As they reach blackout, the curtains on the proscenium stage slowly part, revealing the interior of the stable beneath the Inn. The rear wall of the stage is completely plain. This is so that it may be lighted near the end of the scene and act as a cyclorama against which the final action will

135

be silhouetted. *Before this wall are five uprights spaced about four feet apart and reaching eight to ten feet in height. Across these five uprights is a horizontal bar, set in three sections, but made to appear as one long timber about six feet above the floor, as shown in Figure "A" below.*

There is a manger affixed to the center upright. (See Fig. a. Mary is asleep on the mound of hay just to the right of the manger. To left and right, near the wings and well upstage, are either cribs of hay or piles of hay (depending upon available properties) and life-size cutouts of cows, sheep, donkeys may be placed about. These will add much to the final silhouetted scene.

To stage right is a wall with a small window with bars. It should be about shoulder high. Simulated moonlight shines through it. Joseph stands, silently looking out into the night, moonlight illuminating his face.

To stage left is a practical, "Dutch-type" door that can be opened. (Joseph opens the top half only when the shepherds first come.) The lighting is a mixture of pinks and blues to simulate a night scene, but bright enough to reveal facial features.

Along the rear wall, hidden behind at least a foot high masking flat, or other suitable obstruction, is a row of blue lights, strong enough to flood the rear wall evenly. (See Fig. b)

(As the curtains part, voices are heard outside the stable door. Joseph glances toward the door, then down at Mary as she stirs and sits up.)

MARY: *(Sleepily)* What is it, Joseph?

JOSEPH: *(Kneeling beside her and placing his hand on her shoulder)* Probably someone bringing animals into the stable.

MARY: But why do they knock? Could it be Roman soldiers?

JOSEPH: Roman soldiers don't knock. Perhaps the Innkeeper told whoever it is that we were here and they are showing us a courtesy by knocking before coming in. I'll see who it is.
(Joseph rises and crosses to the door. He opens only the top half. We hear voices from without, at first.)
Yes, what is it?

SHEP: *(From outside the door)* Are you the husband of the woman who is heavy with child?

JOSEPH: *(Guardedly)* Why do you ask?

SHEP: *(Quickly)* We mean no harm, sir. We are but shepherds from the nearby hills. We must know . . . was your wife delivered of her child tonight?

JOSEPH: *(Puzzled)* Yes . . . about two hours ago.

SHEP: *(Now, excited)* Did you wrap Him in swaddling clothes and place Him in a manger?

JOSEPH: But . . . how could you know? No one has come into or
     left the stable from the moment we entered!
SHEP: It was revealed to us in a vision, sir.
JOSEPH: A vision?
SHEP: Yes.
JOSEPH: *(Opening the bottom half of the door)* What kind of a vision?
     Come in!. . . . Come in!
SHEP: *(Entering slowly, followed by other shepherds. They enter and
     stand quietly inside the door.)* It happened about the third watch.
     Suddenly an angel appeared in the sky above us! He told us not
     to be afraid . . . that he had a message for us. Then he said
     how we would find the Savior of Israel . . . Christ the Lord . . . in
     Bethlehem, wrapped in swaddling clothes and lying in a manger.
     All at once the whole sky was filled with angels, singing! The
     words were, "Glory to God in the Highest! Peace on earth and
     good will to men!"
JOSEPH: *(Quickly turning to Mary)* Mary! Did you hear? The Lord
     has sent us a sign! At last, after all these months, He has sent us
     a sign! *(Turning to the shepherds who have remained in the door-
     way)* God has brought you to us!
SHEP: Then you believe us?
JOSEPH: *(Very excitedly)* Believe you? Oh, God be praised . . . yes,
     I believe you! *(Indicating the manger)* Come . . . see for yourself
     . . . here is the Savior of Israel . . . just as the angel told you!
     *(The shepherds slowly approach the manger. As they near it,
     they remove their headgear and kneel before the manger)*
SHEP: *(To his son)* Come Nathanial, this is the night that you will
     never forget, for here is the promised Redeemer of Israel!
BOY: *(Approaching the manger)* But father . . . our King born in a
     stable?
SHEP: *(Placing his hands on his son's shoulders)* Many great men of
     Israel were born in humble surroundings, my son. Moses was
     cast adrift in a small boat. David was but a tender of sheep, even
     as you. God, in His own way, has raised up many humble men for
     mighty works.
BOY: I understand, father. Perhaps I might even march in His great
     army. *(He kneels beside his father at the manger. There is an-
     other loud knocking at the stable door.)*
INNKEEPER: *(From outside the door)* I'm sorry that I must bother
     you, but there are three men of great wealth who insist on my
     awakening you. Will you open the door?
JOSEPH: *(Hurrying to the door)* One moment . . . I am coming.
     (Joseph opens the door and the Innkeeper comes in.)
INNK: *(Entering)* I'm truly sorry to bother you at this time of. . . .
     *(He sees the shepherds and stops in mid-sentence; then, indig-
     nantly.)* See here, now! I offered the stable to you, but now I find

137

it filled with many others! By what right have you brought . . .

JOSEPH: *(Quickly interrupting)* Sir . . . they arrived but a moment ago. They are not staying. They have come only to see our son. He was born but a short time ago.

INNK: *(Satisfied)* I'm sorry, sir . . . I spoke in haste. So, your wife did have her baby this night . . . and it is a son? *(To Mary)* Are you all right? You should have sent for my wife.

MARY: You are very kind, sir. There was no need to bother you. There is my son, all snug and warm in your manger . . . thanks to you.

INNK: *(Looking at the manger)* He's a handsome one! My wife will be very pleased to know that the swaddling clothes did come in handy. If there is anything we can do . . . *(Suddenly remembering)* What am I thinking of! There are three men . . . *(Meaningfully)* . . . and very wealthy men, I might add, who wish to see you. Were you expecting them?

JOSEPH: *(Puzzled)* No . . . we weren't expecting anyone. Are you sure they haven't made a mistake?

INNK: Well . . . now that you mention it . . . they didn't seem too sure. They just asked if there were anyone here with a new baby . . . that is, a boy baby. When I told them about your wife being very near her time, they insisted upon seeing you.

JOSEPH: I'm sure they must be mistaken. . . .

SHEP: *(Interrupting)* Sir . . . could it be that they also saw a vision?

INNK: Vision? What vision? *(Quickly)* Aah! I haven't time to worry about such silly superstitions! I have to get back to my guests! Do you, or don't you, want to see these men?

JOSEPH: Yes. Send them down.

INNK: *(Heading for the door)* Oh . . . they're right outside. *(Turning at the door and speaking to Mary)* My wife will be glad to come if you need her. *(To Joseph)* I'll send them right in.

MARY: *(After he is gone)* Joseph! I'm worried.

JOSEPH: *(Reaching for her hand)* Now, there is nothing to fear. If they meant any harm, they would have come right in. Anyway . . . these shepherds will help us if we need. . . .

SHEP: *(Stepping forward)* You needn't fear, ma'am . . . we will . . .

(He falls silent as the three wise men enter. The first one steps forward a pace of two, while the other two stand silently by the door. The shepherds draw back to stage right and stand quietly alert. Joseph steps forward.)

JOSEPH: I don't know for whom you are looking, but my wife and I have never known anyone of your evident importance. I'm sorry that you have wasted your time, for I'm but a carpenter and we have come down from Nazareth to register for Caesar's taxation. we are strangers in Bethlehem.

138

MELCHIOR: *(Stopping Joseph with a raised hand . . . then speaking kindly)* May I make myself and my two companions known to you? This is Casper, my dear friend. *(Indicates Casper)* And this is Balthazar another old friend. *(Indicates Balthazar)* I am Melchior. We have come a long way in search of him whom the Scriptures speak of as King of the Jews! The Innkeeper informed us just now that a son was born to your wife this night.

JOSEPH: Our son was born not two hours ago.

MELCHIOR: Then the star has led us aright! *(Turning to his companions)* Our long journey has ended.

JOSEPH: A star?

MELCHIOR: *(Turning back to Joseph)* Yes . . . we have followed a star and it led us here. Just this night it came and stood above this Inn. May we see the child?

JOSEPH: These shepherds were also led to this Inn . . . but by the words of an angel. Now you have come, following a star. I know that God's hand must be over it all. Come . . . our son is in this manger.

(Joseph moves over to Mary's left and slightly upstage, and to the right of the manger. The shepherds are behind him and farther to the right. The three Wise Men come slowly to the left of the manger and look down. As they see the baby for the first time, all three slowly kneel. Melchior lifts his hands upward and looking toward heaven, he speaks.)

MELCHIOR: Blessed be the Lord God of Abraham, Isaac and Israel, for this night we have seen Messiah. . . . Praise His Holy Name and may the purpose of His coming be fulfilled in all nations!

(Melchior then faces front and claps his hands three times, slowly. Immediately two bearers enter with a trunk-like container and set it down in front of Mary and to her left. Melchior kneels before the container, opens it and places gifts before Mary.)

CASPER: *(Speaking as Melchior places the first gift)* I offer to Messiah, frankincense. May His life, as it is offered for His people, be a sweet savor of redemption rising before the throne of His Father!

BALTHAZAR: *(Speaking as Melchior places the second gift)* I offer to Messiah, myrrh. Even as its substance is harvested through great pressing of the vine, so it symbolizes the agonies of Messiah's Kingship.

MELCHIOR: *(Speaking as he places a third gift before Mary)* I offer Messiah, gold. It is refined to perfect purity and is the symbol of the purity and Kingship of God's Holy One! May His reign be eternal!

(As the three gifts have been placed, the three men move to

139

the left of the manger. Casper kneels beside and to the left of the manger, while Melchior and Balthazar stand immediately behind him.

The shepherds press forward to form a picture. The manger is in the center with Mary and Joseph to its immediate right. Mary is seated, looking down at Jesus and Joseph stands immediately behind her. The shepherds are kneeling or standing to make an appropriate silhouette. Slowly the frontal lighting begins to fade, and all characters "freeze" in their positions, not moving at all. Only the blue lights lighting the rear wall are left on, and the soft yellow light from within the manger which indicates the child Jesus. As the frontal lights fade, leaving a silhouetted tableau of the "Creche" scene, a voice is heard singing the first verse of "O Holy Night" by Adam. As the refrain, "fall on your knees" begins, the uprights and cross bars of the left and right stables are allowed to slowly drop away to the left and right, leaving the central upright and cross-bar, in the outline of a cross, rising above the manger. (See Fig. a.)

At the end of the verse, the curtain slowly closes on this scene.

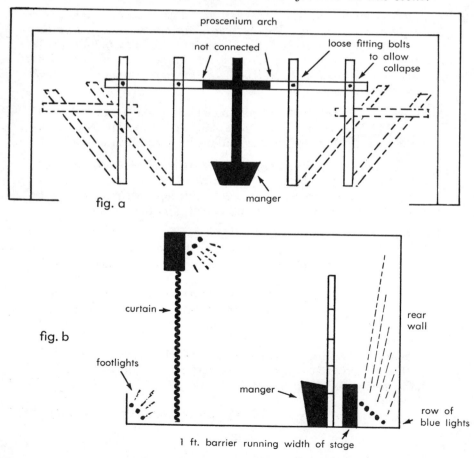

fig. a

fig. b